Chasing Rainbows

Paula Jeffery

Chasing Rainbows

Copyright © 2011 Paula Jeffery

All rights reserved

ISBN: 1461149266

ISBN-13: 978-1461149262

Dedicated to

Graham Jeffery

for his unending patience, support and love

Chasing Rainbows

Contents

Introduction	9
Early Rainbows	15
Double Rainbows	29
Joseph Rainbow	33
James and Sarah, silk weavers	36
Jabez rainbow	47
Cast list of trial	58
The Journey	73
Life in Van Diemen's Land	79
Married Life	85
The Tickner Murder Mystery	88
The Brundles - the next generation?	91
Dying Young	94
An Actor's Life For Me	105
The enigma that is Lillie Blanche Rainbow	121
Osmond Tearle	125
Edwin Rainbow	133
Henry Rainbow	143
Amy Alice Watts Rainbow	145
William Ballard Rainbow	149
Percy Rainbow	157
Leonard Rainbow	165
Patricia Rainbow	170
Other Researchers	175
Appendix	181
Obituary of Joseph George Rainbow 1839 - 1893	182
Obituary Henry Rainbow 1833 - 1913	184
Obituaries of Edwin Rainbow	188
With love from Daddy	194
Bibliography	211

Chasing Rainbows

Acknowledgments

My sincere thanks to Lynne Dady and Janet Kidner, my proof reading team for picking up my grammatical errors and particularly for their dedicated work with commas; to Cotesbach Educational Trust for generous access to their archives; to my mother, Patricia Sanders (nee Rainbow) for sharing her photo stash and enduring 'the interview'; to Thomas, Philip and Nicola Jeffery for asking polite questions and not glazing over (too much) when answered; to Roger Waeckerle for online support and encouragement and of course to my husband Graham, for reading, re-reading, suggestions, cups of coffe and just about everything else.

Chasing Rainbows

"If you cannot get rid of the family skeleton, you may as well make it dance."

George Bernard Shaw

INTRODUCTION

Researching family history is the ultimate never-ending task. Occasionally I sit back, cast an eye over the boxes and files and decide I've come to a natural conclusion and that it's time to put it all down on paper in neat chronological order. Then snippets of additional information surface or more genealogical records are made available on the Internet and the chase begins again. It's taken a while but I've gradually come to realise that my work in this area will never be 'complete' and I need to get everything recorded before my notes (and brain) get too old, crumpled and indecipherable.

My prerogative as narrator of this family tale is to start with me, Paula Jeffery (nee Sanders) born smack bang in the middle of the nineteen fifties, June 1955. An early interest in family history was sparked by Nan and Pop, my maternal grandparents Leonard and Hilda Rainbow. During a period of my childhood we all lived together, my parents and younger brother Mark, along with my grandparents in what were to be the 'Devon folly years' - an aspiration of an idealised extended family living together in a rural, seaside paradise. Inevitable inter-generational and financial tensions led to the ultimate failure of the dream and a return to the city in the early 1970s, but it was fun while it lasted.

It was during the Devon years, as a young child, that I would launch myself into Nan and Pop's bed on wintry weekend mornings, cuddling down between them and begging for a story about 'when you were little'. I would drink in tales of mischievous brothers playing tricks in outside toilets, spinning tops and pigs carcasses hanging from hooks in the scullery ceiling. My grandparents were both born during the first decade of the 20th century and their childhood world, which existed with no inside bathroom or television, seemed a million miles away from my thoroughly modern 1960's experience. Nan would tell me all the funny and slightly naughty tales from her schooldays. Pop was slightly disapproving, I imagine not wanting to encourage rebellion in his favourite (and only) granddaughter. He told me about his own granddad, Edwin who seemed to have been a rather grand but kindly old man who would take Pop on jaunts into Coventry town centre when he was a 'nipper'. Edwin would wear a top hat and be constantly pulling out and checking his gold pocket watch.

When I was older Pop told me that genealogical research of the Rainbow branch of our family had been undertaken by some unknown relative; that this mysterious researcher had discovered we were descendants of French Huguenots and that the Rainbow name itself was originally the French version of Rainbow, *Arcenciel*. This sounded glamorous enough to merit further investigation and I have to say, at this juncture, and many years later, I have neither proved nor disproved either of these facts, but I have uncovered a lot more.

It was natural for me to take the Rainbow line as my main genealogical interest, partly because it seemed such an uncommon name that I thought it would be easier to find information. I have branched out to explore other lines but for now I'll stick with the Rainbows. They're enough on their own!

As well as being an endless task, family history is also messy. Where do we start to tell the story? At the earliest information and work forward? Do we branch off and include information about cousins or stick rigidly to the one line? Father to son? Start at the end and work backwards? Again, which road should we travel? I've chewed over this problem far too long and here's what I've finally decided to do; I'm going to write about the individuals that I know most about, in roughly chronological order. I'll tell their stories and include chopped up family tree diagrams so you can see where they fit. I'm not going to be too dogmatic about following a direct line. If they're a 3rd cousin, twice removed or even an acquaintance or work colleague and they have an interesting story, they're in! My aim is to find a balance between the pure facts: date of births, deaths and marriages and the fascinating stories that drop when you begin to shake the tree a little. I've recently discovered that this form of genealogical research even has a name, cluster genealogy - when you include the siblings, neighbours, employers and friends of direct ancestors. I don't feel quite so disorganised now it has a name!

Over the years my family history journey has taken many twists and turns. I started casually in the late 70s, gathering a few birth, marriage and death certificates, talking to older members of the family and moved on to sitting in libraries for hours on end poring over microfiches of census returns and old newspapers. Then along came the Internet with rudimentary genealogical websites and message boards until now when we have so much digitised information available to us it can be a little overwhelming. There have been the Eureka! moments, for example, the first time I had access to the *Times Digital Archives*, casually typed in Rainbow and emerged a couple of hours later having found a 'missing' great, great, great, great uncle and began to piece together an extraordinary story of attempted murder and intrigue. It's interesting to note that at that time (2004) there wasn't anything like the general interest in genealogy there is today, only six years later. Searching for "Jabez Rainbow" on internet search engines in those days drew a complete blank and now there are various websites mentioning the most notorious of the Rainbow ancestors, and some even have the correct information! I feel rather like a pioneer saying that when I first found out about Jabez I had to organise for a researcher in Tasmania to photocopy his convict records and send the information by 'snail mail' and now all the convict documentation and Australian newspaper archives are online - it's made research so much simpler and faster.

During my studies I've also realised that there is a lot of inaccurate information floating around, particularly on the Internet so I've tried to verify everything I've found with reputable sources such as birth, death and marriage certificates and census returns. I'll try to include every source of information if possible. If there is an ambiguity or I'm making a supposition I'll mention that its guesswork and if you're interested enough you can follow it up and prove me right (or wrong!)

I hope this information may be of use to anyone who's looking for information about members of the Rainbow family in particular or just a general interest in genealogical research. I know I've been grateful for a couple of roughly scribbled down family trees by ancestors who've trodden this long and winding road before.

As the saying goes, all human life is here from criminals to churchmen, from weavers to actors, from passive resistors to soldiers and all the rest of us in between.

One of the frustrations with digging up the family tree is that there is much more information about the famous or infamous but very little about the 'ordinary' working man or woman. I would have loved to have found more information about the everyday lives of our ancestors, not just the ones who made the headline but unfortunately little evidence is available. Forgive me then, if large portions of this book are unfairly devoted to a handful of Rainbows - all a little bit famous for very different reasons.

Chasing Rainbows

EARLY RAINBOWS

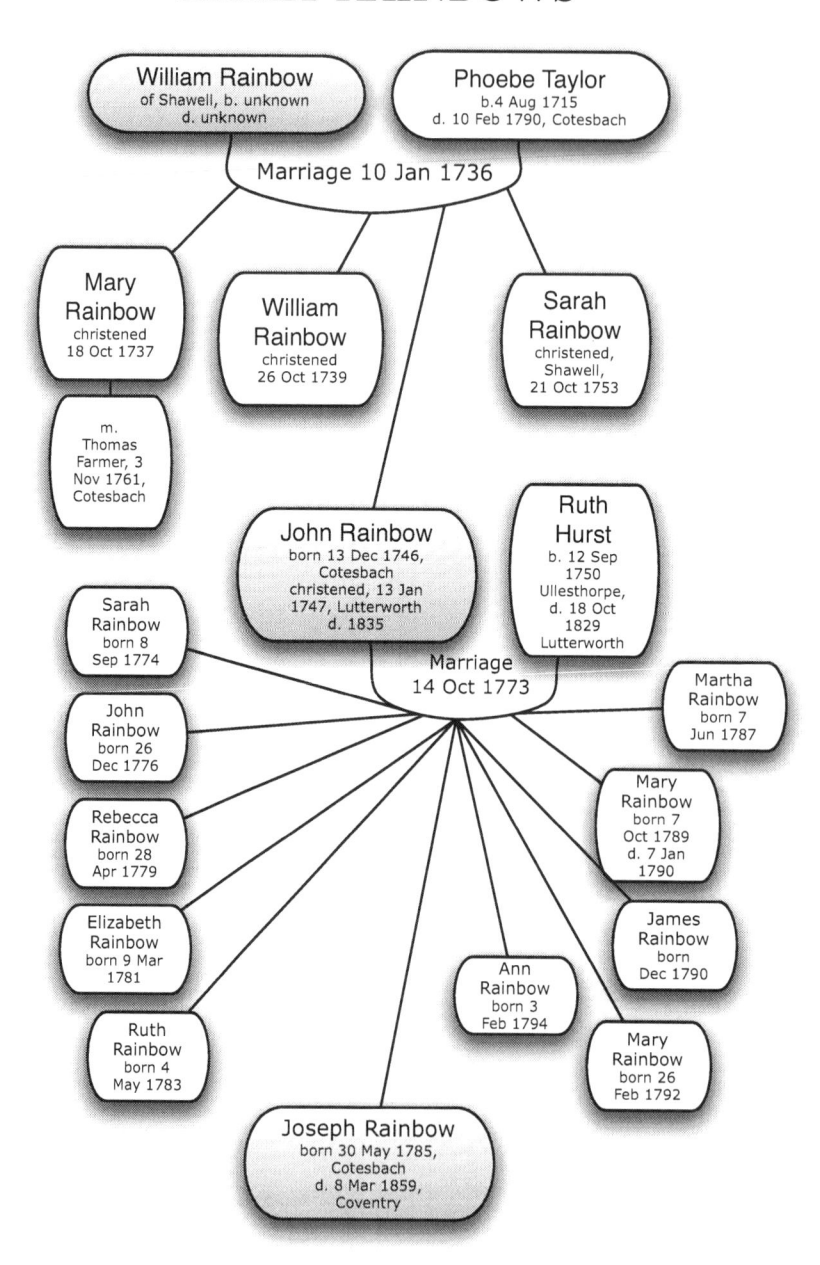

William Rainbow
of Shawell, b. unknown
d. unknown

Phoebe Taylor
b. 4 Aug 1715
d. 10 Feb 1790, Cotesbach

Marriage 10 Jan 1736

Mary Rainbow
christened 18 Oct 1737

m. Thomas Farmer, 3 Nov 1761, Cotesbach

William Rainbow
christened 26 Oct 1739

Sarah Rainbow
christened, Shawell, 21 Oct 1753

John Rainbow
born 13 Dec 1746, Cotesbach
christened, 13 Jan 1747, Lutterworth
d. 1835

Ruth Hurst
b. 12 Sep 1750 Ullesthorpe,
d. 18 Oct 1829 Lutterworth

Marriage 14 Oct 1773

Sarah Rainbow born 8 Sep 1774

John Rainbow born 26 Dec 1776

Rebecca Rainbow born 28 Apr 1779

Elizabeth Rainbow born 9 Mar 1781

Ruth Rainbow born 4 May 1783

Joseph Rainbow born 30 May 1785, Cotesbach
d. 8 Mar 1859, Coventry

Martha Rainbow born 7 Jun 1787

Mary Rainbow born 7 Oct 1789 d. 7 Jan 1790

James Rainbow born Dec 1790

Mary Rainbow born 26 Feb 1792

Ann Rainbow born 3 Feb 1794

Early Rainbows

"They never show you this part on *Who Do You Think You Are*[1], do they?" said the woman at the record office, laughing, as she fought to load up a reluctant microfilm reel on the machine next to mine. She was right; although the TV programme has popularised genealogy like never before, all the tedious work that underpins genealogical discoveries has magically been completed by the archive fairies aka BBC researchers before the celebrity sits in the record office to 'ooh' and 'ah' at the results before the camera. The frustration is missing.

One of the classic obstacles with genealogical research is hitting the 'brick wall'. Typically this happens when a point is reached where we can't research back any further because of missing or non-existent records. Civil registration - the legal requirement of a government to record all births, marriages and deaths - only began in the UK in 1837 and before that point the family historian largely relies on parish registers for information. The availability of these church records varies considerably and unless we find a family connection that taps into a well researched lineage such as a royal or aristocratic family we have to accept the inevitable that written records will run out sooner rather than later.

I may have reached that point with William Rainbow.

Over the years I've worked back through the generations via the male line of Rainbows and eventually ended up at William. He's the earliest Rainbow I've found, so far, and after countless raids on the archives I haven't been able to find his birth record and consequently, information about his parents. My hope is that his family originally

---

1   British genealogy television documentary series that has aired on the BBC since 2004. In each episode, a celebrity goes on a journey to trace his or her family tree. The series has spawned several international versions including US and Canadian editions.

came from Bedfordshire or Northampton. There were large families of Rainbows based in these areas in the 16th and 17th century and the lazy researcher within me thinks it would be wonderful to link in with these already well researched families. As it stands I've come to a full stop with William.

William married Phoebe Taylor on 10th January 1736 in the tiny village of Shawell, Leicestershire, about two miles south of Lutterworth. I have seen information suggesting that William was born in 1720 but I haven't been able to find an actual record of his birth so this is pure speculation and sixteen does seem a little young, for a boy in particular, to marry.

William and Phoebe had at least four children, Mary (1737), William (1739), John (1746) and Sarah (1753) who were all born in Cotesbach, another small village in the same parish, where the records indicate that the father of the children was 'William Rainbow of Shawell.'

John Rainbow, the youngest son of William and Phoebe, is the child that is the direct ancestor to my branch of the Rainbows. He was born on 13th December 1746 in Cotesbach. To put his date of birth into context, George II was on the throne and it was the year Bonnie Prince Charlie fled to the Isle of Skye after the Jacobite Rising and the Battle of Culloden. John Rainbow, married Ruth Hurst on 14th October 1773 and according to parish records they had eleven children between 1774 and 1794 with at least one child dying in early childhood. Mary Rainbow was born in 1789 and died barely three months later.

I have scant knowledge about the rest of the children apart from my direct ancestor Joseph Rainbow, John and Ruth's sixth child who was born on 30th May 1785 in Cotesbach and christened at Lutterworth Independent Church.

Parish records of births, deaths and marriages are available for the area that go as far back as 1558 (currently held at Leicester Record Office, Wigston) and although they are on microfilm, the sixteenth century handwriting and deterioration of the original records makes deciphering them difficult. The only other birth, death and marriage data I have discovered about the couple is that Phoebe died, in Cotesbach, on 10th February 1790.

View from the schoolroom on the Cotebach Estate.

The schoolroom was purpose built in the late 18th Century, by Rev. Robert Marriott, for the education of the children of Cotesbach and the surrounding villages.

Reproduced with kind permission from Cotesbach Educational Trust

The village of Cotesbach has an interesting history being famous as the gathering place for the Enclosure Riots of 1607. These riots took place around the country as the landowning gentry began to enclose land traditionally left available for villagers to graze cattle and/or grow crops. Villages became depopulated as the inhabitants were no longer able to support themselves and this came to a head in Cotesbach when a reported crowd of 5,000 people gathered to protest and physically level the enclosures. The alleged ringleader was hung for treason and although this was largely a non-violent protest the resulting riot a week later at Newton in Northamptonshire saw 40 protesters massacred after a proclamation by King James I ordering the protests to be suppressed. Perhaps not surprisingly, this reduced the rioting considerably. By 1609 Cotesbach was partially enclosed and by 1612 it was fully enclosed.

In 1759 Cotesbach Estate was purchased by a Robert Marriott from Braunstone, Daventry; the acquisition included the living (a church office endowed with fixed capital assets that provided a means of income) and the estate, consisting of all the property in the parish, every house and every acre of land, a circumstance, commented on in The Gentleman's Magazine (April 1860), that happened only rarely. Along with his purchase of the estate Marriott also acquired the advowson; the right to nominate a person to hold a church office in the parish. Following his ordination, aged 27, Revd. Robert Marriott, became rector of the parish of Cotesbach and remained incumbent from 1768 until his death in 1808. The estate has remained in the custodianship of the Marriott family until the present day.

Cotesbach itself may yet yield more information about the Rainbows who lived there. In September 2010 the Cotesbach Hall Estate hosted a Heritage event and I went along on a day that promises to mark a turning point in the search for more information about the earliest of this particular branch of the Rainbow family.

The Estate holds rare, if not unique, treasure in the extensive estate records spanning 250 years that have lain, undisturbed for decades. These include 18th century account books, over 500 handwritten sermons, personal letters, recipes, maps and newspaper clippings -

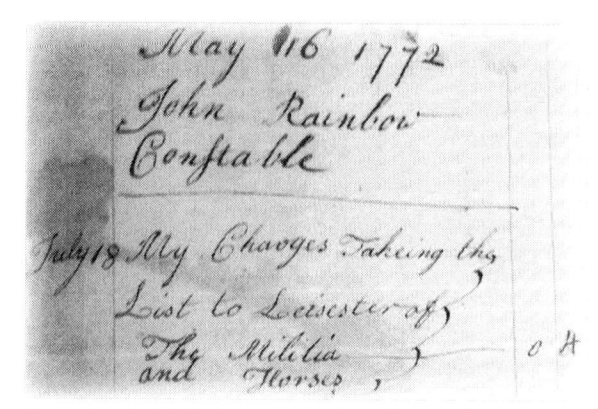

Reproduced with kind permission from Cotesbach Educational Trust

a microcosm of social history contained in one house. These are to be on permanent loan to the Cotesbach Educational Trust and are in the process of being catalogued with the aim to make this valuable information available to all.

Imagine my delight on discovering that Rainbow was already a familiar name with the custodians of the collection. William Rainbow and his son, John, feature in the records with both father and son holding tenancies on the estate as farmers and/or graziers.

An 1804 map shows the fields that John farmed and an account book details the rent paid for each field. There is also an indication of an earlier generation of Rainbows in the Cotesbach/Shawell area. On a map dated 1720 one of the fields is marked as 'Rainbow'. If we consider that William Rainbow married in 1736 and that this was his first marriage, we could speculate that it is unlikely that he would have been farming on his own account in 1720.

As well as being farmers, father and son also held 'official' positions within the parish. In a Cotesbach estate account book dating from the mid 18th century William Raynbow (note the spelling) is recorded as Overseer of the Poor in 1764 and further down the same page as Constable. A few pages later, in 1772, John Rainbow is listed as Constable. These offices were important positions within the community and the information could also give us a clue about the date of William's death. It is possible to speculate that William is likely to have died at some point between 1764 and 1772 with son, John taking over the role of Constable from his father.

Power in the parish

An Overseer of the Poor was an elected position within the parish and was required by law. Before the Reformation in the sixteenth century it was considered the duty of every Christian to perform the Seven Corporal Works of Mercy:

- Feed the hungry
- Give drink to the thirsty
- Welcome the stranger
- Clothe the naked
- Visit the sick
- Visit the prisoner
- Bury the dead

When Henry VIII denounced the Catholic Church and the Church of England was established these traditional values and moral expectations were seen to be less important and it was felt there was a need to legislate to alleviate the growing problems caused by poverty. Laws were introduced to enable the documentation, control and provision of help to the poor during the sixteenth century including the introduction of parish registers, the authorisation and empowerment of Justices of the Peace and an obligation to categorise the poor as either deserving and undeserving. The deserving, i.e. those who were unable to work because of ill health, age or infirmity were to be given help in the form of 'outdoor relief' which meant that they were given money to survive and remained in their own homes, rather like a 'dole'. The undeserving, i.e. those who could but would not work were to be whipped through the streets until they learnt the error of their ways. In 1572 the first law was introduced which made it compulsory to pay a local poor law tax; the relief of the poor was made a local responsibility and in 1597 the position of Overseer of the Poor in each parish was created.

Every Easter elections were held from 'substantial householders' and approved by two Justices of the Peace. Once elected as Overseer it was almost impossible to refuse the position without a very good reason. Although it was an unpaid post there were often unofficial perks such as grazing rights. The responsibility of an Overseer included setting and collecting the poor rate from residents and distributing the poor relief amongst the needy of the parish. They could also organise apprenticeships for poor and deserving children of the parish and they worked closely with the local Church Wardens.

It is not hard to imagine that this situation was fraught with possibilities both of corruption on the part of the officials and opportunities for the recipients of the poor tax taking advantage of those parishes that were known to be generous. To alleviate the latter, The Settlement Act of 1662 allowed poor relief only to established residents of a parish. If a pauper applying for relief could not prove an association with a parish either by birth, marriage or apprenticeship they were sent to the parish nearest to their birthplace, or where they could prove some connection. On their journey to their 'home place' each parish they passed through was obliged to give them food and shelter for at least one night.

Although the role of a local Overseer of the Poor was despotic it was believed that a locally based official who knew the Poor Relief applicants personally would be able to differentiate between the deserving and undeserving.

The Constable would enforce orders from the Overseers of the Poor and Church Wardens and in parishes with a small population it was not unusual for the same person to fulfil more than one position in the community. A Constable would also be responsible for collecting bastardy payments, dealing with beggars and maintenance of the village 'punishment' equipment such as stocks, pillories and the village lock up. This was also an unpaid position but constables were allowed to claim expenses and the estate records at Cotesbach reveal these expenses in some detail, for example:

July 18th 1772 reads, under a list headed,

'John Rainbow - Constable'

My charges taking the list to Leicester

The Militia and Horses - 4 shillings

John RAINBOW

Genfile

Profile

In brief

John Rainbow, farmer, grazier and carrier born in Cotesbach, Leicestershire, 1746. Died in 1835. Father of eleven.

Known for...

being Constable in the parish of Cotesbach and one of the founding members of the Lutterworth Independent Church

Events

Year	
1772	First mention of John Rainbow, Constable in Cotesbach Estate accounts books.
1773	John married Ruth Hurst from Ullesthorpe and the following year their first child was born.
1793	Appointed Overseer of the Highways for Cotesbach parish.

These records, detailing all collections, expenses and relief for the poor from every parish were required to be submitted to Parliament.

Overseer of the Highways

In 1555 The Highways Act gave the responsibility for the upkeep of the country's highways and byways to each parish and this formed the basis of a law governing road maintenance that would last for nearly 300 years.

On 22nd September every year the constables, tythingmen, churchwardens, surveyors and householders of the parish were required to meet in church and assemble a list of names of at least ten people living within the parish who were qualified to be given the appointment of Surveyor of the Highways. The eligibility criteria was to own land valued at £10 by the year, to possess a personal estate to the value of £100 or to be occupiers or tenants of houses and land with a value of £30. This list was then passed to the Justices of Peace at the Special Session held for highways and a suitable surveyor was duly appointed.

This was an offer that couldn't be refused. The appointment was obligatory.

> *"If any of the said persons so appointed, whose names were contained in such list, and who are served with the said notice, shall refuse or neglect to appear at the said Special Sessions, and accept said office...within six days after being served with such warrant of appointment...he shall forfeit the sum of £5"*

It would appear to have been a thankless task. The surveyor had to ensure that all able bodied parishioners provided 6 days labour, as required by law. He had to check that the work was carried out and that adjacent land owners kept their hedgerows and trees from overhanging the road and their ditches clear. If he was aware of a wagon or cart breaking the law in relation to how many horses or oxen it was pulled by he was required to stand up in church, after the Sunday sermon and announce the name of the culprit in order that they could be prosecuted.

Detailed records were required to be kept and examined by the justices of the peace three times a year. There was no obligation on the parish to keep records for more than one year and many have been destroyed. However, Cotesbach is fortunate to have the accounts book of the Overseer of the Highways from 1786 to 1817 which contains many details of road work carried out in the parish.

Information is included about the levy that was collected, although it isn't clear if this was from individual householders or the turnpikes that had become established during the eighteenth century.

Several men in Cotesbach were Overseers of the Highways between 1786 and 1817, including John Rainbow. It's possible that the later appointment, in 1815, could have been John Rainbow, jnr who would have been 39 years old.

William Armson 1786

John Hill 1787 – 1792

John Rainbow 1793 - post 1796

John Amner 1806

John Rainbow 1815

William Armson 1817

The records reveal how much a team of men and horses were paid for a day's work, that stone was carried from Crick to make and maintain the road at Cotesbach, and that 'ale for the men' could be included in expenses.

Intriguingly I have also discovered a law book from 1823 which details an appeal against a sentence with regard to the case of Rex v the inhabitants of Cotesbach. The villagers were indicted by another parish for not repairing the roads. Cotesbach Estate, as far as we know, doesn't have any records for the repairing of roads after 1817 and I haven't been able to find details of the actual court case.

Further information from the Cotesbach archives [2] reveals that towards the end of his life John Rainbow was being paid a regular sum of £4 11s at roughly six month intervals from the autumn of 1832 until June 1835, with a final payment to his daughter, Elizabeth Bradford (nee Rainbow) of £5 in July 1835. There is no indication of what these payments were for. John was buried in Lutterworth on 4th June 1835; he was 88 years old when he died. We could speculate that the payments may have been some kind of pension with a final payment of a round figure to cover his funeral costs or possibly as a mark of appreciation.

We may assume from this information that, at least these two generations of Cotesbach Rainbows were respected members of their community, both literate and holding elected official positions.

Although John features in the Cotesbach archives I have limited information about William's other children, Mary, William junior and Sarah. Mary Rainbow married Thomas Farmer on 3rd November 1761 in Cotesbach, and was recorded in the parish records as 'daughter of William Rainbow.' Unfortunately Farmer being such a recurrent surname in Leicestershire at that time I haven't been able to trace descendants but there were no persons with the surname Farmer living in Cotesbach in 1841. At the time of writing I have no further information on William Rainbow, junior or Sarah apart from the dates of their births/baptisms.

Non-conformists

There is a certain mystery as to why two generations of Rainbow children who were all born in Cotesbach were baptised in Lutterworth when there was a parish church in both Cotesbach and Shawell. There

---

2 (COTMA:2010.656)

also appears to be no Rainbows buried in Cotesbach, (although there were several Rainbow weddings).

Lutterworth Independent was the non-conformist church in the neighbouring town. Although there had been a parish church since the fourteenth century in Lutterworth, the political, social and religious upheavals of the seventeenth century that led to the Act of Uniformity in 1662 caused a split. This law required that all churches used and adhered to the Book of Common Prayer. The ministers that were not prepared to conform to this edict were expelled from the church. This led to the formation of informal gatherings of worshipers at private houses and later formal breakaway churches being founded. In Lutterworth a group of dissenters formed the Church of Christ in 1689 where the present United Reform Church, which was built in 1777, stands today. The church website lists the names of the early trustees noting that 'in the main, they were prosperous country folk, e.g. John Rainbow, Grazier of Cotesbach.' From the scant information it's difficult to tell what time period this refers to and to ascertain which John. William's son John Rainbow, was born in 1746 and baptised at 'Independent, Lutterworth' on 13th January 1747. John's son (also John) was born in 1777, however as John Rainbow junior is listed as a carrier in Lutterworth in the 1841 census and they are referring to 'early trustees' it is probably safe to assume that one of the founders of the current United Reform Church in Lutterworth was John Rainbow, senior.

Chasing Rainbows

DOUBLE RAINBOWS

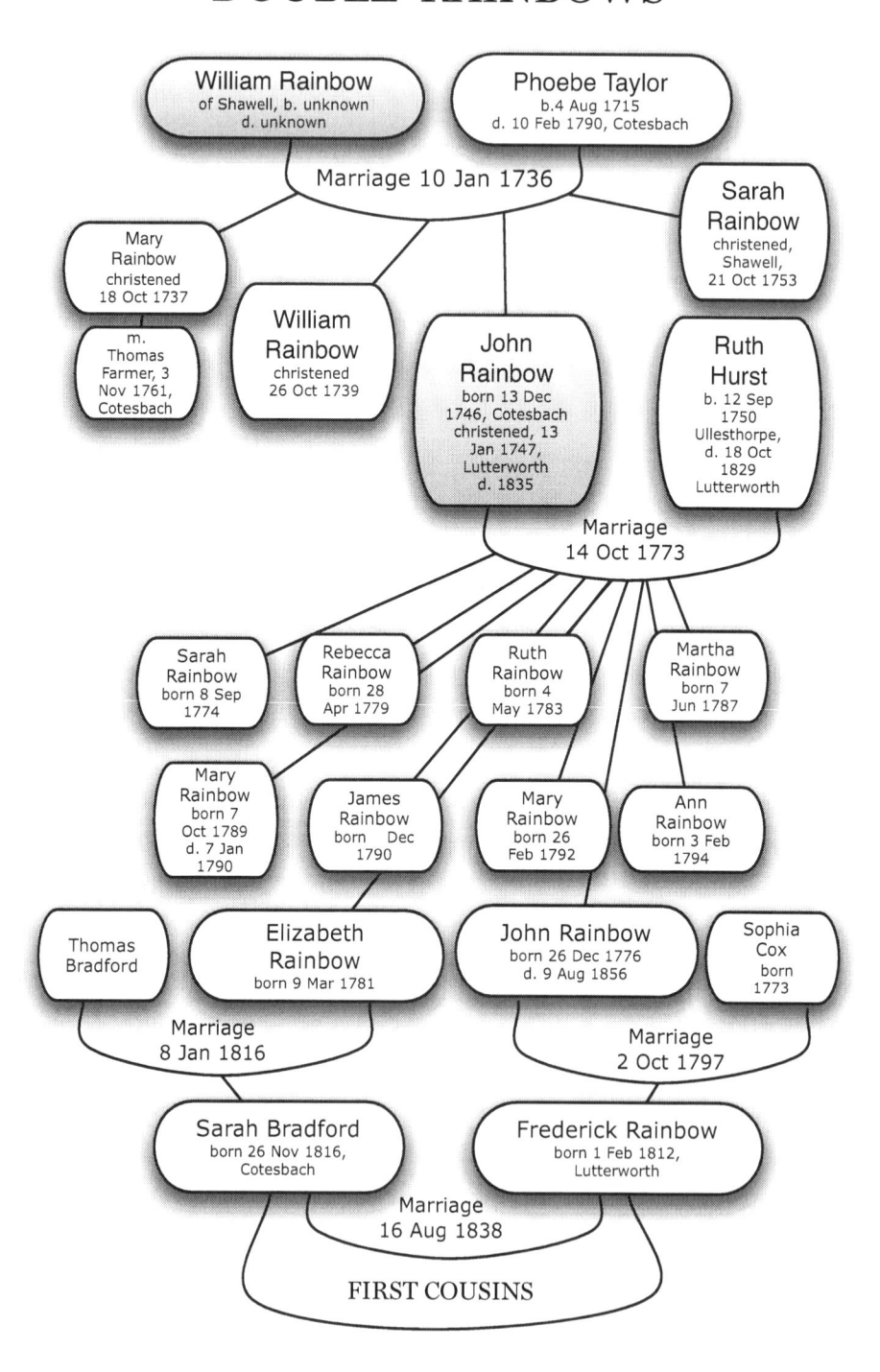

William Rainbow of Shawell, b. unknown, d. unknown

Phoebe Taylor b. 4 Aug 1715, d. 10 Feb 1790, Cotesbach

Marriage 10 Jan 1736

Children:
- **Mary Rainbow** christened 18 Oct 1737 — m. Thomas Farmer, 3 Nov 1761, Cotesbach
- **William Rainbow** christened 26 Oct 1739
- **John Rainbow** born 13 Dec 1746, Cotesbach, christened 13 Jan 1747, Lutterworth, d. 1835
- **Sarah Rainbow** christened, Shawell, 21 Oct 1753

John Rainbow m. **Ruth Hurst** (b. 12 Sep 1750 Ullesthorpe, d. 18 Oct 1829 Lutterworth) — Marriage 14 Oct 1773

Children:
- **Sarah Rainbow** born 8 Sep 1774
- **John Rainbow** born 26 Dec 1776, d. 9 Aug 1856
- **Rebecca Rainbow** born 28 Apr 1779
- **Elizabeth Rainbow** born 9 Mar 1781
- **Ruth Rainbow** born 4 May 1783
- **Martha Rainbow** born 7 Jun 1787
- **Mary Rainbow** born 7 Oct 1789, d. 7 Jan 1790
- **James Rainbow** born Dec 1790
- **Mary Rainbow** born 26 Feb 1792
- **Ann Rainbow** born 3 Feb 1794

Thomas Bradford m. **Elizabeth Rainbow** — Marriage 8 Jan 1816
→ **Sarah Bradford** born 26 Nov 1816, Cotesbach

John Rainbow m. **Sophia Cox** (born 1773) — Marriage 2 Oct 1797
→ **Frederick Rainbow** born 1 Feb 1812, Lutterworth

Sarah Bradford m. **Frederick Rainbow** — Marriage 16 Aug 1838

FIRST COUSINS

28

Double Rainbows

Family connections get more complicated and enmeshed with the next generation of Rainbows. John and Ruth's daughter, Elizabeth Rainbow married Thomas Bradford in Cotesbach in 1816 and seems to be the last remaining Rainbow in the village as she appears, on the 1841 census, aged 60, Elizabeth Bradford, a chandler living alone in Cotesbach. Thomas and Elizabeth had a daughter, Sarah Bradford (b. 1816).

John and Ruth's son, the aforementioned John junior, Lutterworth carrier, married Sophia Cox in 1797 and they had six children. Their youngest son was Frederick Rainbow (b. 1812).

In August 1838 Frederick Rainbow and Sarah Bradford, first cousins, married and the first of their six children was born in 1839. All the children were related, twice over, to the Cotesbach Rainbows. I discovered this family of 'double Rainbows' when I found Elizabeth Bradford, aged 70, recorded on the 1851 census. She had moved from Cotesbach and was living with Frederick and Sarah Rainbow in Lutterworth and listed as 'mother-in-law' to the head of household. It took a few minutes of head scratching to work out how Elizabeth, a Rainbow by birth, could be the mother-in-law of Frederick Rainbow.

Kissing cousins

First cousin marriage in twenty-first century Britain is generally disapproved of and even regarded by some as bordering on the incestuous. The practice has been legal since Henry VIII changed the law to accommodate his desire to marry his own first cousin and it was relatively common in the Victorian era. Between three and five percent of the marriages of the aristocracy and landed gentry in the mid to late 19th century involved first cousins, the incidence falling in the general population to about 1.5 per cent. These figures are based on research conducted by George Darwin at the behest of his more famous father, Charles, who himself had married his first cousin and was concerned for the health of his children. Adam Kuper, writes in the New Humanist that after collecting data from wedding announcements, marriage records and questionnaires and gathering statistics from the heads of asylums and other institutions George calculated that the incidence of abnormalities arising from first cousin marriages was about three to four per cent which was not too far out of line with the incidence arising in the general population. According to Kuper, the conclusion of the research indicated that first cousin marriage was not damaging to the offspring of such unions, at least not in the 'best families' with the caveat that it should probably be avoided by the poor! However, even with Charles Darwin himself endorsing the results other research revealed different findings, which resulted in several US states banning first cousin marriage and the practice falling out of favour in Britain after the First World War.

Very little medical information is included amongst census data, particularly the early returns so it is difficult to say if the 'double Rainbows' of Lutterworth suffered any ill effects. I have only scant information about this branch of the family, except that they ran a carrier business in Lutterworth for many years. My principal research interest amongst that generation of Rainbows was John's son, Joseph – the next direct ancestor of our branch of the Rainbow family.

Chasing Rainbows

COVENTRY RAINBOWS

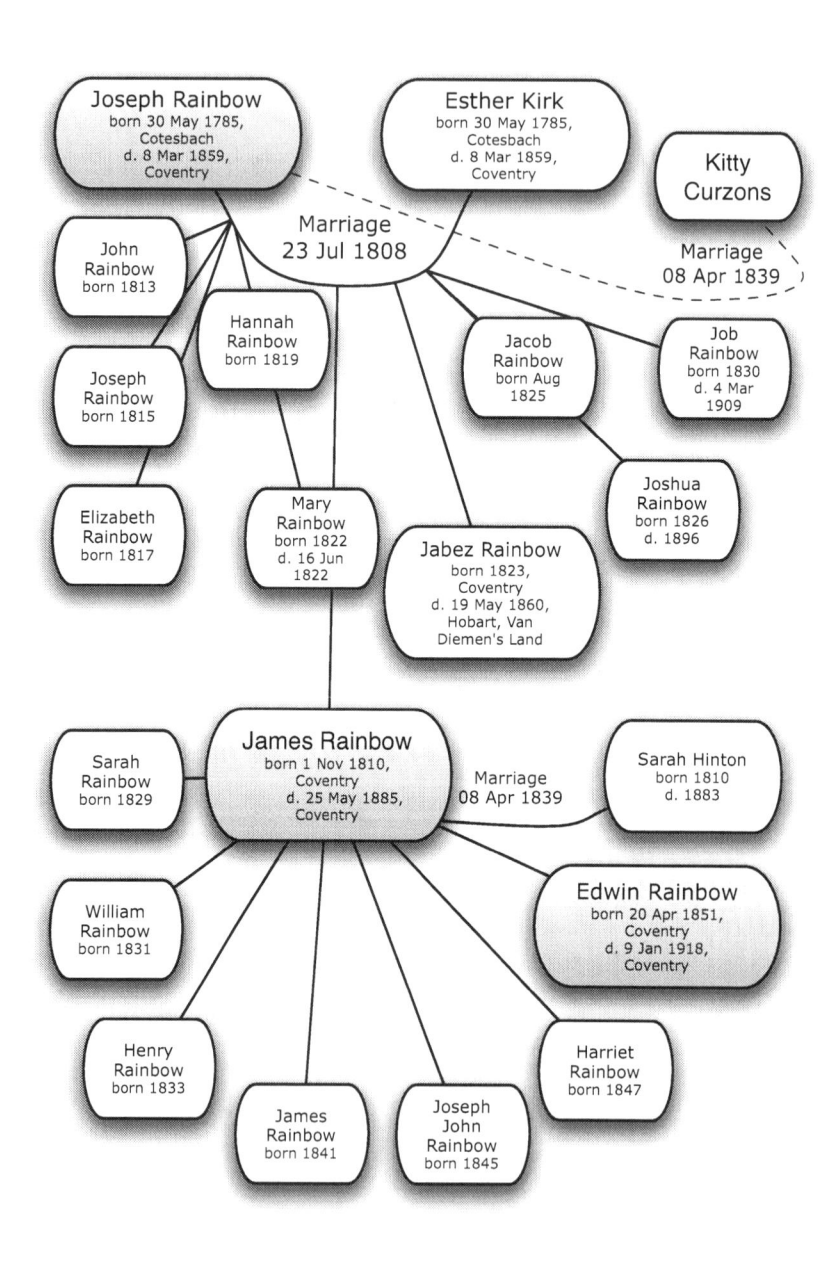

Joseph Rainbow
born 30 May 1785, Cotesbach
d. 8 Mar 1859, Coventry

Esther Kirk
born 30 May 1785, Cotesbach
d. 8 Mar 1859, Coventry

Kitty Curzons

Marriage 23 Jul 1808

Marriage 08 Apr 1839

John Rainbow born 1813

Hannah Rainbow born 1819

Jacob Rainbow born Aug 1825

Job Rainbow born 1830, d. 4 Mar 1909

Joseph Rainbow born 1815

Elizabeth Rainbow born 1817

Mary Rainbow born 1822, d. 16 Jun 1822

Jabez Rainbow born 1823, Coventry, d. 19 May 1860, Hobart, Van Diemen's Land

Joshua Rainbow born 1826, d. 1896

Sarah Rainbow born 1829

James Rainbow born 1 Nov 1810, Coventry, d. 25 May 1885, Coventry

Sarah Hinton born 1810, d. 1883

Marriage 08 Apr 1839

William Rainbow born 1831

Edwin Rainbow born 20 Apr 1851, Coventry, d. 9 Jan 1918, Coventry

Henry Rainbow born 1833

James Rainbow born 1841

Joseph John Rainbow born 1845

Harriet Rainbow born 1847

Joseph Rainbow

Joseph Rainbow was born in Cotesbach, Leicestershire on 30th May 1785, the sixth child of John Rainbow and Ruth (nee Hurst).

One of the earliest indications of where Joseph lived and his occupation was in 1839 when he is recorded as father of the bride on Hannah Rainbow's wedding certificate, living in Coventry and working as 'attorney's clerk'.

Conjuring up an image of a Victorian attorney's clerk it is easy to imagine the pictures painted for us, so vividly, by Charles Dickens. Novels by Dickens contain many examples of clerks, from the good natured and timid Bob Cratchitt in A Christmas Carol, to the creepy Uriah Heep in David Copperfied and the pathetic and vengeful William Guppy in Bleak House. Although these are fictional characters the young Dickens himself worked as an attorney's clerk so we might imagine that his writings might not have veered too far from reality. The duties of lawyer's clerk would have included running errands and the monotonous copying of documents. This was in the days before even the most basic of office machinery such as manual typewriters were in use - it wasn't until 1874 that the first typewriter was available commercially. Every document was drafted and written by hand, including any necessary copies. Searching for Joseph Rainbow in the Coventry archives I found his name appears many times as a witness on official documents such as mortgages and wills. Although not very well paid, this was a 'white collar' occupation, which was suitable employment for the son of a 'wealthy landowner', and he would have been considered 'respectable'.

On 23rd July 1808 Joseph married Esther Kirk at St. Lawrence's Church, Foleshill, Coventry. Esther was a silk weaver living in Coventry and this might have influenced Joseph to settle in the town. This is also the first indication I can find of the family's involvement in the silk weaving industry.

The direct line of this branch of the Rainbow family follows down through Joseph to his eldest son, James, who was born in 1810. He was the first of ten children including seven sons whose names all began with the letter J. James, John, Joseph, Jabez, Jacob, Joshua and Job.

Esther died on 22nd July 1838 aged 51. She left behind Joseph with their youngest child, Job, only eight years old and their daughter, Hannah, aged 19, still at home. Less than a year later Joseph remarried and this may have been the catalyst that set off a chain of events ultimately leading to tragedy.

Joseph spent his life in Coventry and died on 8th March 1859.

James and Sarah, silk weavers

James Rainbow was born in Coventry in 1810, the eldest son of Joseph and Esther (nee Kirk). He was the grandson of John, the elder brother of the notorious Jabez and the father of Edwin.

I know little about his early life except that he completed his apprenticeship as a silk weaver and, at the tender age of 19, on 4th August 1829, he married Sarah Hinton at St. Catherine's Church in Coventry. Sarah was also aged 19 and originally from Shoreditch, London. Their first child, Sarah was born 4 months later, christened on Christmas day and buried just a few days later, on 7th January 1830.

As if this wasn't a traumatic enough start to their married life the next year would bring more difficulties for the two young silk weavers.

A crisis in silk weaving

On 7th November 1831 silk weavers of Coventry numbering approximately 200 men assembled for a meeting to discuss the problems the industry was facing. The focus of their attention was a man called Josiah Beck. He had been born in 1813, a contemporary of James and Sarah, in the village of Ansty, just outside Coventry. He became a successful silk weaver at a time when the industry was on an upswing. Many people in Coventry depended on silk weaving for their livelihoods and earned a very good living. It is maybe a measure of how good this was as a career move when we see that James' father, Joseph, who worked as a lawyer's clerk, a 'respectable' white collar occupation, would choose to put his sons through silk weaving apprenticeships rather than encourage them to take up his own profession.

To maintain these high living standards, silk goods from Coventry were able to be set at a high price as demand outstripped supply.

However, the cotton and wool industries in the north were beginning to become mechanised and mills were being used to supply vast quantities of wool and cotton which made fortunes for the mill owners and decimated the traditional cottage industries.

In 1830 Josiah Beck decided to expand his workshop of six silk weaving hand looms operated by hired labour and installed a steam engine. A drive shaft drove his looms and before long his expanded workshop of ten automated looms was turning out the work of 100 men. The price of silk began to drop dramatically bringing dismay and unrest amongst the silk workers in the town.

An angry meeting took place at 10.00am on that November morning in 1831, at a room in Little Park Street, Coventry. The men formed a committee and agreed to meet again at 3pm. However shortly after the meeting ended a mob of about 700 men gathered and a breakaway group of 500 attacked Beck's factory, at New Buildings. They smashed the looms, threw silks and ribbons from the windows and set the place on fire. They found Beck on the site and beat him violently. He managed to escape on two occasions before the mob finally took him by hand cart back into the town. When the authorities became aware of what was going on the magistrate's clerk was sent to read the Riot Act. The crowd began to disperse as the 14th Light Dragoons and 7th Hussars were sent in to quiet the unrest. The theatre and the pubs were closed and soldiers were placed on guard at factories that were potential targets. Handbills were issued urging 'respectable' citizens to sign up as special constables. By midnight all was quiet and by the morning the ringleaders had been arrested. In March 1832, Thomas Burberry, Benjamin Sparkes and Alfred Toogood were sentenced to death for their part in the riot. However, this caused public outrage and the Crown stepped in and commuted their sentences to transportation for life to Van Diemen's Land. Josiah Beck never prospered again after this incident and he ended his days as a pauper at the Bond Hospital, Coventry.

This all took place 2 months after Sarah and James had their son, William, their first child that survived childhood. We can only speculate about whether James was one of the 700 that day in the centre of Coventry, angrily shouting about the falling silk prices or maybe he was appalled at these actions. Either way the coming of steam would have impacted greatly on what should have been the start of a lucrative career.

Following the unrest of 1830 technological advances in silk weaving in Coventry were delayed with even forward-looking employers understandably nervous of implementing a full factory model. The Cash brothers sought a compromise by building individual cottages for their workers and powering the looms in each house with one steam engine. This allowed the weavers to keep their independence but proved uneconomic as the power had to be supplied even if the looms were not being worked.

In 1841 James and Sarah were living in Gosford Street with sons, William aged nine and Henry aged seven. James was a ribbon weaver and they had Mary Crofts, aged 14 living with them, a ribbon weaver's apprentice. This would indicate that ribbon weaving was still a viable occupation for the family in 1841.

In 1851 the family were living at 111 High Street, Coventry. James and Sarah were both 40 years old and they are listed as ribbon weavers. Living with them are their son William, aged19, Henry aged 17, both ribbon weavers, James aged nine who 'turns a winding wheel', Joseph aged 6 and Harriet, 4. They were all recorded as being born in Coventry except for Sarah who was marked as N.K (not known). Maybe Sarah was not up to answering questions about her birthplace. The census that year took place on 31st March and Sarah would give birth to her last child, Edwin less than three weeks later on 20th April.

High Street, in the heart of the city, is probably one of the oldest roads in Coventry and was part of the main thoroughfare going from east to west. At the time of writing it is the home to various building societies and banks but in 1851 it was at the centre of the ribbon weaving trade; three neighbours living on each side of James and Sarah were all employed in the ribbon trade as weavers or silk winders.

The beginning of the silk weaving industry in Coventry is said to date back to the fleeing of refugees, the Protestant Huguenots, from France in the 1600s who were escaping persecution by the ruling Catholics. Mainly skilled craftsmen and women they settled in communities around Europe with 50,000 arriving in England and they were generally welcomed by the local population for their expertise in trades such as weaving and watch making.

By 1821 in Coventry one in four of the population were involved with silk weaving and because of overcrowding within the city walls a settlement was created, mainly for silk ribbon weavers, at Hillfields, north west of the town centre. This became home to the skilled craftsmen and women, living in purpose built residential property with gardens and a 'top shop' to house one or more looms. A typical home would consist of two rooms and a scullery on the ground floor with two bedrooms upstairs. A top storey housed a workshop that spanned the whole floor, a ladder being used for entry. Large windows for maximum light stretched from floor to ceiling.

Although ribbons form an insignificant part of the fashion industry in the twenty-first century, for Victorian ladies with their ornate dresses and bonnets the addition of the perfect ribbon embellishment could make an outfit. Most ribbons were made from expensive raw silk with both silk and patterns being imported from France. Jacquard looms meant that highly patterned ribbons could be produced made possible by Joseph-Marie Jacquard's invention of the first programmable loom using cards punched with holes. The perforated cards passed over needles and activated the threading system whenever a needle passed through a hole. The holes determined the pattern of the weave. This was the first practical use of the binary system and the pre-cursor of computers, which probably makes silk weavers the first geeks!

Some Coventry weavers were outworkers for 'masters' - the raw silk would be weighed and collected at the factory and the 'undertaker' would expect to receive ribbons of the same weight in return. No matter how hot the workroom became in the summer windows were kept closed, as the fresh air would dry out the silk, making it lighter. Likewise even in the harshest winters no fires were allowed on the top floor because of smoke tainting the precious silk. Weavers typically worked sixty hours a week, taking snacks at the loom with one main meal in the evening. Poor light from evening work using gaslight and repetitive movements in cramped conditions led to eyestrain, backache and associated injuries. Although the housing may have been purpose built there was no drainage or sewerage system in the town. Water had to be fetched from a pump at the top of the street several times a day and sanitary utilities consisted of an open pit situated near to the house into which all manner of offal and rubbish were thrown. The filthy conditions led to several outbreaks of epidemics such as cholera and it wasn't until as late as 1858 before a sewage system was established in the town.

Family split

In the 1861 census I was surprised to find that James was not living with Sarah. She is listed as married and the head of the household at 162, Queen Street, Coventry with James 19, Joseph 16, Harriet 14, and Edwin aged 10. Living in the same house and also listed as head was Job Rainbow. Job was James' youngest brother, twenty years his junior being born in 1830. He was living with his wife also named, confusingly, Sarah (nee Green), Josiah their son aged 3 and their daughter, Sarah Elizabeth aged one. Sadly Sarah Elizabeth was to die the following December. All the adults were involved in the ribbon weaving industry as weavers or winders, except for James junior, who was a watch finisher. I was puzzled by the non-appearance of James senior on this census. I knew he hadn't died because on the future censuses, James and Sarah were back living together in Coventry. Searching further on the 1861 census I found a James Rainbow living in London. He was listed as a 'servant & ribbon weaver', born in Coventry and was staying with his sister-in-law, Ann Hinton a coffee house keeper at 94, St. Martin's Lane, London. All this information fits in with our knowledge of James and Sarah (nee Hinton), the only fly in the ointment is that his age is listed as 30 instead of 50 but taking all the other evidence into consideration I'm fairly confident this is our James and that the age difference was a census enumerator's error.

It also fits with Coventry's prevailing economic climate and the critical slump in the weaving industry in 1860/61.

Boom and bust

Coventry has a history of being a 'boom or bust' town, experiencing waves of good fortune followed by years of financial depression. Watch making, bicycles and motor manufacturing have all given the town vibrant if short-lived prosperity and silk weaving was no exception.

In 1860 the Cobden Treaty was ratified which removed the tariff from French silk goods resulting in the silk market being flooded with cheap imports and making it difficult to export home produced silk ribbons. Around the same time the fashion for ribbons began to fade to be replaced by feathers and the USA imposed duty on British made ribbons. All these factors contributed to the decimation of the ribbon industry in Coventry. Small home based producers were not able to survive, leaving a few large factories to weather the economic storm. In a last ditch attempt to save the trade the silk masters began to ignore the set price, which resulted in a devastating strike and lockout. Many weavers emigrated and this is most likely the reason that James was living in London in 1861. It would appear that the family were pulling together to help each other out during tough times with James working as a servant in his sister-in-law's coffee shop and the families of the two Rainbow brothers sharing a house.

Although the modernisation of the industry began after 1861 weavers continued to fall in number and silk weaving began its slow decline.

Joseph Gutteridge

A contemporary of James and Sarah was another Coventry silk weaver, Joseph Gutteridge, who had an interest in mechanics and natural history and published his autobiography about his life as a weaver, *Light and Shadows in the life of an Artisan*.

Although I have no evidence that James and Sarah had any connection with Joseph Gutteridge we might assume that as a contempory of our Rainbows, in the same town and working in the same trade he may have shared similar experiences.

Born in 1816 Gutteridge apprenticed as a weaver at the same factory where his father worked. He had an impulsive romanticism and married before he had completed his seven-year term and had been able to buy his own loom. Politically he was a Liberal and a moderate. Even though he and his family suffered severe hardship during the 1840s and again in the 1860s, along with the rest of the Coventry weavers, he was slow to blame the government's policies.

A man of principle or stubborn bordering on the foolish, depending on your viewpoint, Gutteridge refused to accept aid available to freemen of the city who had fallen on hard times. Even though his wife and children were starving he declined because it would have meant affirming religious beliefs that he, at this period in his life, no longer believed in.

In 1867 Napoleon III opened the Paris World Exposition. 52,000 exhibitors from 41 countries contributed to the theme, The History of Labour. The exhibition attracted more than eleven million visitors and was held on a site that covered an area of 119 acres. 6,000 of the exhibitors were from Britain and the Society of Arts chose a group of artisans to visit the exposition and report back on their findings. One of those chosen was Joseph Gutteridge, who represented the ribbon weaving trade. In his report he commented that the British goods that were displayed were the normal output for everyday sale contrasting them with the French goods that were made especially for the exhibition. He was impressed by the intricate fabrics that had a 'special character' and would require 'extreme manipulative skill' to produce. He was so impressed that he travelled to St. Etienne and Basle to see for himself the machinery that had produced such work and he reported that he found 'at each place machinery of the most intricate complication used in the manufacture of ribbons, silks and velvets, such, indeed, as we in Coventry could have no conception of.' He remarked that the foreign machines were adapted to clear, size and prepare the silk and the weaver has little to do but concentrate on the weaving. He saw the European methods as giving the French and Swiss great advantages over the Coventry workers and made a strong case for improving technical education in England in order for the local weaver to become more competitive. Gutteridge was very appreciative of the generous hospitality offered by the manufacturers in St. Etienne and Basle particularly as when French and Swiss delegates had visited Coventry in the past they had been refused admittance to some factories.

Gutteridge clearly saw the failure of the silk weaving industry in the UK as largely the fault of a technical and skill deficit amongst British workers rather than a political failure. This did not go unnoticed with the prime minister of the day, William Gladstone. Gladstone had co-authored the Cobden Treaty, which had dealt the killer blow to Coventry weavers so it would make sense that he would be heartened by a silk weaver who was apportioning blame to other factors rather than blame the treaty for the demise of the industry. Gladstone kept a copy of Gutteridge's book in his library and also arranged for him to be paid £70 from the Royal Bounty fund.

Back with the Rainbows, the weaving industry in Coventry continued to limp along. In 1871 James and Sarah were living at 70, East Street, Coventry, both listed as silk weavers aged 60. Edwin was still at home, aged 19 and was working as a printer's apprentice.

By the time of the 1881 census Edwin had married and had left home. James and Sarah were alone, aged 70 and living at 12, Weston Street, Coventry. They were still both listed as silk weavers with Sarah's place of birth being 'Middlesex, Shoreditch'. It has occurred to me that there is a possibility that Sarah Hinton is the ancestor that comes from a Huguenot background in silk weaving. Even though James's father, Joseph was a lawyer's clerk and his father John was a farmer the story of the Rainbows originally being descendants of

Huguenot silk weavers has persisted down through the generations. We know that Huguenots flocked to Sarah's home place of Shoreditch in large numbers establishing a major weaving industry in and around Spitalfields. I haven't been able research Sarah's family any further at the time of writing because there are many, many Sarah Hintons from around that time in the Shoreditch area, but it would be an explanation of what, so far, appears to be a family myth. There are several references in obituaries that the Coventry Rainbows were from an "old silk weaving family" and maybe that refers to Sarah Hinton or even her mother-in-law, Esther Kirk.

James and Sarah Rainbow both lived to be 73. They died in first half of 1883 within a few months of each other.

Chasing Rainbows

Genfile

Jabez RAINBOW

Profile

In brief

Jabez Rainbow, born in Coventry 1832, died Van Diemen's Land, 1860. Son of Joseph and Esther Rainbow.

Known for...

attempting to murder his girlfriend, Jane Pearce at The Boot, St. Albans in 1841.

Events

Year	
1841	Jabez was a silk weaver's apprentice and ran away to join the army.
1842	Sentenced to be transported to Van Diemen's Land for 15 years after cutting Jane's throat.
1848	Married fellow convict, Eliza Maycock

Jabez rainbow

In the first flush of family history research it seems natural to work back through the generations as directly as possible. This typically means from grandfather to great grandfather and back via the male line with barely a scribbled note of siblings along the way, these are not our 'direct' ancestors, after all and if the 'bloodline' is all important they often receive only a sidelong glance as we push on to find earlier generations. It is perhaps only when we hit a brick wall and can't go back any further that the siblings of younger ancestors begin to get some attention. In my case this is where some of the most interesting stories have been discovered.

I can't remember exactly when I first saw the name Jabez Rainbow but I was undertaking some rudimentary detective work early on in my family history search when I tracked back from Edwin to his father, James and noted down a handful of James' siblings. I gathered together the dates of birth, marriages and deaths for completeness, but apart from birth, christening and a record of his indenture as a silk weaver's apprentice, I could find no other data relating to Jabez. There were no details of a marriage or a death, neither locally nor nationally. It did occur to me that he had left the country and I tried a superficial search of emigration records and passenger lists. Nothing. He'd vanished.

Several years later, in 2004, I signed up to take a short course with the Open University called Start To Write Your Family History. The course was fascinating in itself but more importantly it gave me access to The Times Digital Archive, a searchable, full text facsimile of every issue of the paper published from 1785 to 1985. This proved to be a treasure trove of information including a clipping about a certain Jabez Rainbow. The story originated from St. Albans during the latter half of 1841. My initial reaction was to discount the report as I knew there were a large contingent of Rainbows living in the south of England during the nineteenth century and this was likely to be that branch rather than one of 'our' Rainbows. However, the story continued for several editions and on into 1842 and more information was revealed. It stated that Jabez was originally from Coventry and a runaway silk weaver's apprentice. He had been using the alias of Kirk since he absconded. Our Jabez Rainbow was Coventry born, a silk weaver's apprentice and his mother's maiden name was Kirk. Bingo!

Jabez was born in Coventry, in 1823, the eighth of ten children born to Joseph and Esther Rainbow. At the age of 14 he began an apprenticeship with Isaac Molesworth, a silk weaver from Silver Street, just a few streets away from Cow Lane where the Rainbow family lived. In 1838, when Jabez was fifteen his mother died and the following year his older sister, Hannah, married. Three weeks after Hannah's wedding his father, Joseph married Kitty Curzons, a fifty-year-old weaver. We could speculate that Hannah was likely to have been caring for her younger siblings after her mother died and when she married and left the family home Joseph needed a replacement to care for his remaining children. Kitty had never married and lived just a couple of streets away in Freeth Street. As an aside, also at this time and living in Freeth Street were a certain Jeffery family, also silk weavers and the direct ancestors of my husband, Graham. Genealogy certainly throws up some strange coincidences!

When Jabez was indentured for his seven-year apprenticeship, Joseph must have thought that his son was set for life with a good trade under his belt. Coventry was enjoying all the advantages brought about by the boom years of the silk weaving industry, as mentioned earlier. Jabez though, had other ideas and he was almost halfway through his term when he ran away to join the Army. A statement from a recruiting sergeant of the time said that craftsmen such as weavers, only applied to join up when they were in trouble. However, I can find no record of any other earlier crime being committed by Jabez. The use of his mother's maiden name as an alias might indicate he had something to hide but it may have been simply to avoid detection as a runaway apprentice. Absconding was a serious crime punishable by hard labour.

So this is where Jabez found himself, apprenticed to a silk weaver in the summer of 1840 and who knows what was going through his mind on that June 18th day when he ran away and joined the 34th Regiment of the Foot. Did his mother's death and his father's subsequent remarriage drive him away? Or were the conditions of his apprenticeship unbearable? Little is known about his time as a new recruit except that he enlisted using the name Jabez Kirk and was initially stationed in Dover.

Army life

Whatever the motivation for Jabez to run away, if he imagined that an Army career was a more attractive option than weaving silk, he was going to be in for a shock. Life as a Victorian soldier was tough.

At that time the public tended to look down on military men; they were assumed to be criminals or at the very least ruffians. Soldiers were often recruited from rural areas where work was hard to come by; the army preferring the physically stronger and eager to work country boys to the streetwise apprentices and factory workers of the towns. Young men found guilty of minor crimes were often given the choice of a term in prison or joining the army. Up until 1847 signing up meant signing up for life to a rigorous and often brutal life where flogging was common for even minor misdemeanours until it was banned in 1881. Rather like the misplaced pride of young men who have received an ASBO[3] in 21st century Britain, some regiments referred to themselves as 'redbacks' boasting of their toughness at being able to withstand repeated whippings.

The barracks that greeted a new recruit to the army were described at the time as only ranking 'with asylums for the insane or some of the new poorhouses'. The barest of bare essentials were provided. An oblong room with a door at one end and a fireplace at the other

3   Anti-Social Behaviour Order

with iron bedsteads running down each wall that folded up during the day and a few tables and benches. Washing facilities consisted of no more than a pump in the yard with the Ordnance department not yet sanctioning 'water closets.'

Overcrowding frequently occurred with sometimes twice the recommended number of men living in the cramped space. A commanding officer described one barrack room that was thirty foot by twenty foot and housed sixteen men. One halfpenny candle was supposed to light the room and the small fire was only able to heat five of the occupants at any one time.

'Through The Ranks to a Commission' by John Edward Acland-Troyte is an insight into life in the Victorian army. Acland-Troyte was an Oxford graduate who had left it too late to pursue an immediate commission in the Army; instead he was encouraged to enlist as a regular soldier and work his way up the ranks. He joined in 1873, some thirty years later than Jabez, and of course changes to military life will have occurred during that period. However, we might assume that his description of his first experience of barrack-room life may well have been recognisable to many soldiers throughout the Victorian period, including Jabez:

> *"The room I was to occupy was on the ground floor, very lofty and well ventilated, three large windows and a good fireplace. Barrack-rooms are all furnished much alike; and I may as well describe them at once, to show what my new home was like. The walls were whitewashed, and the floor bare boards; there were tables in the centre, sufficient for all the occupants of the room to sit down to at once, and wooden forms to correspond. Generally a hanging shelf over the table, on which are kept all the plates and basins, one of each being provided for each man in the room. The iron bedsteads are arranged all round, the heads against the wall, and they are made in two parts, so that during the day one half can be run in or closed up under the other, thus giving much more free*

space to move about it. The mattress is rolled up, pillow inside, and kept fastened with a strap, the two blankets and two sheets folded up very neatly and placed on the top of the rolled mattress, which is stood against the head of the bed, occupying about half of the bedstead when closed up. The remaining half (on which the rug or counterpane is laid) serves for the men to sit on. As a rule there is a space of about three or four feet between the bedsteads, and a man next a window is generally better off.

All round the rooms, over the heads of the beds, are iron shelves, and hooks just below, each man having that part of the shelves immediately over his own cot. All the soldier's worldly possessions are kept on these shelves, and have to be arranged with scrupulous tidiness. The knapsack and other accoutrements are put on the hook, and the rifle generally stands in a little place made for it close to the head of the bed. Very often if a man has near his cot a piece of spare wall he will hang up pictures which gives the room a more comfortable appearance, and provided it is done tidily it is never objected to.

The other articles of common property in the room are a hair broom, mop, long handled scrubber (for cleaning the wood floors) a hand scrubbing brush (for cleaning tables and forms), two tin dishes, on which the dinner is brought in, two tin pails, two wooden buckets, and a big iron coal box, also two coal trays, ie square wooden boxes used for carrying coal about in but generally kept in the room for throwing litter into. The neatness of the room depends chiefly upon the sergeant in charge. If he is a good man he is most strict in enforcing the old rule, "A place for everything and everything in its place" and the men soon get to learn that this is really for their own comfort. The men also pride themselves in keeping things clean and bright, especially if they ever get praised by the officers inspecting the room. The tables are often quite beautifully white; and without plenty of hand-scrubbing they soon get a very different colour; for all the meals take place on them without tablecloths, and ink may be spilt, etc or they may be spoiled in many ways. As a rule the men keep one side of the table extra clean. To explain this I ought to say that the regulation barrack-room table is made in 6 foot lengths, each length being supported by and merely resting on two iron trestles; so that the table can be used with either side uppermost, or can be taken off the trestles and stood against the wall, which would be done always when the floor was swept or washed. The "extra clean" side of the table would only be seen on special occasions, such as the officers visit to the room, and kit inspections, etc. At all meals the side least clean would certainly be used. The tin dishes and cans also get their full share of rubbing, until they quite shine again."

John Acland-Troyte's experience may not have been typical. He says himself that "the colonel had sent me to the company commanded by his best captain and the captain had put me in the best room". However his description of the practicalities of daily life in the Army are fascinating. He describes his first day with the regiment and walking into the barrack-room.

"I put on my cheerful face, and walking in found what was, for barracks, quite a scene of confusion. It was the day of 'refilling the masses' and a very disagreeable day it is generally voted to be. Soldiers' bedding is all changed periodically. The usual programme on these occasions is as follows: Each solder carries his mattress and bolster to some appointed place, and there rips open one side or end, to empty out the old straw which has probably become, by frequent lying on, small and soft. Later on in the day, when clean cases have been served out, the men are turned into a yard, where the fresh straw has been placed, and there they fill their mattresses and bolsters (a very amusing scene sometimes) the 'old hands' taking

> *care to put plenty of straw, more in fact, than is at all comfortable for the first few nights, for they know well that it will rapidly diminish in bulk. They make their way to the barrack room, where needles and thread are produced, the mattress cases neatly sewn up and a good deal of kneading and beating into shape ensues to make the beds as comfortable as may be for the first night."*

Acland-Troyte continues,

"I was very much surprised on first joining to see how much cleaning and polishing etc was necessary. Men seemed always at it. They did not seem to mind doing it; and I fancy it is a very good thing that they have some useful occupations, for a private soldier has plenty of spare time. The word they apply to this part of their life shows what they think of it, for they always call it 'soldiering'. On a wet afternoon, or when a man has nothing else to do, he will light a pipe, sit down on his cot, and give out to his comrades that he means 'to do some soldiering'."

In the 1840's the daily pay for a soldier was 1s 1d (5½p), (the extra penny had been added on in lieu of beer in 1800), and the deduction for food was 6d (2 ½ p). A soldier couldn't be charged more than 6d for rations but he was reimbursed if food was in plentiful supply and cheap. Generally supplies were of poor quality and monotonous, with little to no vegetable or dairy produce. The ration was 1lb of meat and 1lb of bread a day consisting of two meals, breakfast and lunch. It was claimed that the 34th Regiment of the Foot were the first to introduce a third meal of a cup of tea or coffee and bread in the evening. This was implemented partly to reduce drunkenness - something to "line the stomach" before embarking on an evening's drinking. The practice was swiftly taken up by other regiments and became mandatory for all Army units in 1844.

At some point before the autumn of 1841 Jabez was sent from Dover to join a recruiting party in St. Albans. It is speculation that this was designed to be a stopgap as the majority of the regiment were in Canada. They sailed back from Quebec, arriving in Gosport,

Hampshire on 20th June 1841 and moved to Portsmouth in September of the same year, although Jabez never got to join them.

Recruitment into the Victorian army often involved drink. A 'bringer' or 'crimp' approached young men in public houses at the end of evening when they had spent all their money on beer and encouraged them to join the army.

The bringer/crimp was a freelancer who touted around the town looking for likely men and would then receive a tip from the recruiting party for procuring and handing over a potential recruit. Landlords of pubs would allow their premises to be used by recruiters and they would also receive a payment for their trouble. The would-be soldier would be entranced with tales of the money, travels and women to be had in the army and the temptation of an immediate payment for joining up may have been hard to resist for an inebriated young man with no money in his pocket. However, the story of the 'Queen's (or King's) shilling where a man was committed to the army once he had accepted the coin was largely a myth. New recruits had a cooling off period of four days in which to change their minds although one wonders how easy this would have been in practice.

Acland-Troyte describes this cooling off period as a *"...rule made, I believe, to prevent recruiting sergeants getting hold of men unfairly, and to give the youthful adventurer an opportunity to thinking over the step he has taken. Of course there is a possibility that he may take himself off, but a notice is given to every recruit, at the time of his enlistment, informing him that if he does not come back for the purpose of being taken before a Justice, either to be attested or release himself of this engagement, he will be liable to be punished as a 'rogue and a vagabond'. For a man can change his mind after receiving the shilling, and escape the service by paying one pound called 'smart money', before actually being attested. After that he is bound for the term of his engagement and cannot leave without a proper discharge, obtaining permission from his commanding officer and paying down a sum of money varying according to the length of his service, but never exceeding twenty pounds"*

One can imagine that in practice the ordinary recruit who was tempted by the 'queen's shilling' when drunk and out to impress his friends or a girl would be unlikely to have the means to pay the 'smart money' in the ensuing day or two after enlisting.

Acland-Troyte wrote,

> *"A recruit is saved a great deal of trouble and worry by going straight to the place where the regiment is stationed, and enlisting there as a Headquarter Recruit. Of course the ordinary class of man would not afford the expense of the journey, but would simply go to the nearest recruiting sergeant he knew of; and he would in the course of a few days be sent off to his regiment or depot, most likely being forwarded with three or four other recruits, some of whom might not be very desirable companions."*

We are unlikely to know for sure which route into the Army Jabez took but it is probably safe to assume that, as a runaway apprentice almost certainly with little money, it was via the pub route. He then would have been faced with a march to the headquarters of the regiment in Dover, an ordeal that would have taken several days. Within six

The Boot - St. Albans

months we know he was stationed in St. Albans and engaged in the act of signing up young men himself in and around the pubs of the town.

Sir Charles Trevelyan described recruitment as taking place in *'the lowest haunts of a town'* with all recruits being drunk when they were enlisted. The potential new recruit was encouraged to lie about his age and marital status and once he had received his bounty money his new comrades would surround him and help him to drink it away. He went on to suggest that the recruiting parties were lodged in the worst houses in town and thus mixed with characters of such depravity they would corrupt even the best of men.

I doubt we'll ever know whether Jabez was a misguided innocent corrupted by the 'low life' he experienced by working as private soldier in a recruitment party or a 'bad lad' made worse by the relative freedom he enjoyed without a family or master to keep him in check. What we do know is that shortly after arriving in St. Albans he met Jane Pearse.

A moment of madness

The next part of Jabez' life is well documented in as much as the newspapers of the day carried the story extensively over the next few months. There is a question as to how accurate these accounts may have been and to assess that we need to bear in mind how Victorian newspapers reported crime compared to the media of today. We may categorise modern 'red tops' as belonging to that particular genre referred to as the gutter press, but in the 1840s almost all newspapers appealed to this desire for sensationalism. Gory descriptions of crimes were commonplace with details leaving little to the imagination and the more violent the crime the more column inches it was given. There appeared to be no consideration given to the notion of a fair trial with character assassination, assumption and gossip commonplace in newspapers even before the accused appeared in court.

Journalism was a relatively new profession and editors, always keen to cut down costs, would employ hack writers, or 'penny-a-liners.' These were often 'serious writers' hoping to earn a crust from journalism to help finance their more serious writing of novels or poetry. As the name suggests they were paid by the line and flowery prose became the order of the day as they looked to increase their revenue. They had no regular income and worked freelance, selling their stories to the morning journals. If a major crime had been committed it was a race to write the column and literally run to the editor's office to get it on his desk first. Such was the rivalry that one newspaper office had to install a locked box with a slot to post the submissions as rival writers would steal each other's copy from the editor's desk in order to eliminate the competition. Fabrication of stories was also commonplace with reports such as a false story of a suicide of an unidentifiable person submitted when real stories proved to be elusive; these were unlikely to be double-checked and provided some income when times were hard.

It is impossible to judge just how accurate the reports are of Jabez and his trial, given that they are rife with speculation and inconsistencies, but the basic facts are clear. On the morning of October 4th, 1841 Jabez attempted to murder his girlfriend, Jane Pearse and was subsequently transported to Van Diemen's Land (Tasmania) for 15 years.

The following is taken from various reports of the trial in *The Times* and other newpapers, beginning with the first hearing on October 5th 1841 up until the sentencing hearing in March 1842.

Cast list of trial

- Jabez Rainbow, accused
- Jane Pearce, victim
- Mr. J. H. Rumball, the Mayor (and magistrate)
- Mr J. T. Lipscombe (magistrate)
- Mr J. Coles (magistrate)
- Mr F. J. Osbaldiston (magistrate)
- Mr J. Kinder (magistrate)
- Mr J. Smith (magistrate)
- Mr Blagg (town clerk)
- Mr Lydekker (prosecuting lawyer)
- Mr C. Jones (defence lawyer)
- Richard Webster (surgeon)
- Mr Scott (Webster's medical partner)
- Robert Thorpe (private soldier)
- Matthew Richardson (corporal)
- Richard Foxall (landlord of The Boot)
- Baron Gurney (judge)

Jane Pearse

Jane Pearse, as far as I have been able to establish, was born in St. Albans. Various sources have suggested different dates of birth but it is probably safe to say she was born in 1821 making her 20 years old when she met Jabez. One entry in the IGI[4] lists a Jane Pearce being born to Sarah and Joseph Pearce in St. Albans in 1821 and by her reported testimony in court she states that she is 20 years old at the time of the incident, in 1841.

---
4 An index of over 90 million names prepared by the Church of Jesus Christ of Latter-day Saints. It gives marriages, births, and christenings in every country of the world.

"The young woman has resided from her infancy with her parents in St Albans and obtained her livelihood from the straw plait trade, until recently when her conduct became irregular. For the last month she was day and night mostly in the company of the prisoner. "(**The Examiner**, *London, England, Saturday, October 9, 1841; Issue 1758.)*

Jane stated that she had known Jabez for about eight months which coincides with his posting to the recruitment party at St. Albans in January of 1841, some nine months earlier. As to her character and conduct, she is variously described as a 'woman of bad character', having 'loose morals' and more directly, as a prostitute. The use of the word prostitute may be misleading as it would seem that this term was occasionally used during the Victorian era to describe any woman who was intimate with a man she wasn't married to, such were the moral mores of the day. The fact that she was with him, almost constantly, for a month would suggest that they were boyfriend and girlfriend, but again that is speculation.

On the night of October 3rd 1841 Jane and Jabez took a room at The Boot public house in the centre of St. Albans. The landlord, Richard Foxhall, said that Jabez was not billeted at The Boot (according to the 1841 census he was staying at the White Lion, a couple of streets away) but the pair had taken a room there on several occasions, the first time being five weeks earlier. This conflicted slightly with Jane's account - she said that the first time she'd stayed overnight at The Boot with Jabez was a week earlier.

Some of the discrepancies between the testimony of Jane and others might again reflect on the prevailing social and cultural morality of the time. In mid Victorian Britain women were expected to be virtuous until marriage - 'a woman's natural destiny'. Working class people were generally afraid of courts and judges, not least for their great power in passing seemingly random, life-altering, sentences. Communities were close knit and reputations could be damaged beyond repair by a newspaper article or court appearance. This is probably worth bearing in mind when we read Jane's statements. I imagine if she was concerned about the intimate relationship she had with Jabez she would want this to be kept as low key as possible and by keeping quiet and giving only positive information about him she may have thought this was the most prudent course of action.

The room at The Boot, occupied by Jabez and Jane that weekend had three beds. According to Jane's testimony they had also stayed there the evening before, Saturday 2nd, and both the other beds had been occupied. Our attitudes to privacy have changed somewhat over the centuries and it was common practice for strangers to share a room when staying at a cheap lodging house or coaching inn during the 19th century. However, on Sunday night Jabez and Jane had the room to themselves. At around quarter to six the following morning Jabez called down to the landlord to bring him beer and ginger beer. Although this might seem to be a strange request at that time of the morning drinking weak beer was accepted as being an appropriate drink for all, including children, given the poor and unsanitary drinking water available in towns. Foxall took the drinks up to the room and Jabez opened the door, dressed only in a shirt and took the drinks. There was no blood on him.

Initial reports then say that at ten to seven, just under an hour later, Foxall heard Jabez call out "Master! Master!" Foxhall was in the bar at the time and went to the foot of the stairs to see Jabez at the top, still with only his shirt on but now covered in blood. When Jabez saw Foxall he shouted "Murder! Murder!" He went on to shout variations of "Call the police, come take me!" Foxall rushed upstairs and into the room to find Jane lying on the bed with her throat cut, bleeding profusely. Some reports mention that Jabez' face was so thoroughly covered in blood that it was almost impossible to make out his features. Foxall asked Jabez how he had "...come to do it?" but Jabez only replied, "Send for the police."

When John Lacy, the police constable, arrived on the scene he was greeted at the room door by Jabez who said, "Lacy, take me, I have cut her throat" and gestured towards Jane, lying on the bed. The policeman's testimony states that Jabez had no shirt on, only trousers and boots and although his upper body was covered in blood, there was no blood on his trousers. This would suggest that he started dressing before the police arrived, no doubt in anticipation of being taken into custody. In another report, Foxall's evidence, describes the two policemen Lacy and Jacques arriving, the latter being immediately despatched to get medical aid. Foxall and Lacy went up to the room to find Jabez putting his braces on. He went on to add that by the position of the woman on the bed it didn't appear that Jabez had injured her further. It appears that Jabez was left alone in the room with Jane during the time Foxall went for help and the police arriving. It would seem extraordinary that the attacker and victim were left alone together; Jabez getting dressed and Jane, to all intents and purposes lying dying on the bed. *The Era* describes the scene with some enthusiasm:

"On entering the room a horrid spectacle was presented: the floor was covered with blood, while the perpetrator of the deed stood at a short distance from the nearly lifeless, mangled body lying upon a bed, the blood flowing copiously from wounds in the throat and several parts of the body" The Era, (London, England) Sunday 10th October 1841

Lacy asked Jabez what he had committed this act with and Jabez replied, "A razor". He asked where it was and Jabez gestured towards the bed. Lacy rummaged around the bedclothes but couldn't find it. Jane somehow found the strength to pull the mattress up a little to reveal its hiding place. She had managed to slip it underneath after Jabez dropped it. Lacy took the razor and later produced it in court as evidence, still covered in dried blood.

Lacy then grabbed Jabez by both wrists and sat him down on one of the other beds. He noted that Jabez was trembling and he asked him if he had any reason to commit the act; he only shook his head. He was asked to produce his shirt and Lacy noted that it was torn and soaked with blood but there were no wounds on Jabez' body.

Jabez begged to be allowed to wash himself and requested that he be conveyed to the station in the best way to avoid the curiosity of the spectators gathering outside. He was allowed to wash but it is not reported on how he was taken to the station.

Once there Jabez apparently appeared to feel faint; he was given some warm brandy and water followed by tea. He regained his composure and read a newspaper. The magistrate was summoned and during the time before he arrived nobody was allowed to speak to the prisoner.

Richard Webster, the surgeon arrived at the crime scene very quickly, shortly before Jabez was taken away. In his evidence, at the first hearing he described Jane's injuries, noting that he believed she could not have inflicted them herself. At first sight, and because of the excessive blood loss he doubted that Jane would survive but on inspection seeing that the carotid artery remained largely intact and by successfully stemming the flow of blood, he was confident that she would recover.

After Webster had given his evidence the case was adjourned and according to the *The Times* crowds of people assembled to witness the departure of the culprit from the Town Hall, and as he passed by they *"uttered aloud their expressions of disgust."*

Interest in the court case was considerable. Large crowds gathered outside the Town Hall before each court session in order to see the victim as well as the culprit. It would appear that what served to entice the crowds was the chance to see Jane in the flesh, a victim of an horrendous crime who had actually survived. Unlike today where time is needed to gather evidence and interview witnesses, trials in Victorian Britain often took place within days of the crime being committed. On this occasion the star witness, Jane, was recovering from her injuries and the surgeon attending her, Mr Webster, refused to allow her to attend court until she was considerably better, leading to several adjournments with the magistrates becoming increasingly frustrated and the gathered crowds leaving disappointed.

Finally on Friday, 29th October, 1841, just 25 days after the attack Jane arrived at court to tell her story. She travelled from The Boot, where she had lived temporarily after the attack, to the courthouse in a fly (carriage). The courthouse and The Boot were situated close together in the marketplace so the necessity for a fly must have either been because her physical condition was so poor or to protect her from the gazes of the crowds thronging the marketplace. "... much excitement prevailed in the town for a considerable period before 12 o'clock, the hour fixed on for the commencement of the proceedings."

Jane had been lucky on the morning of the attack. Not only because Jabez' razor had missed the vital artery but also because Mr Webster

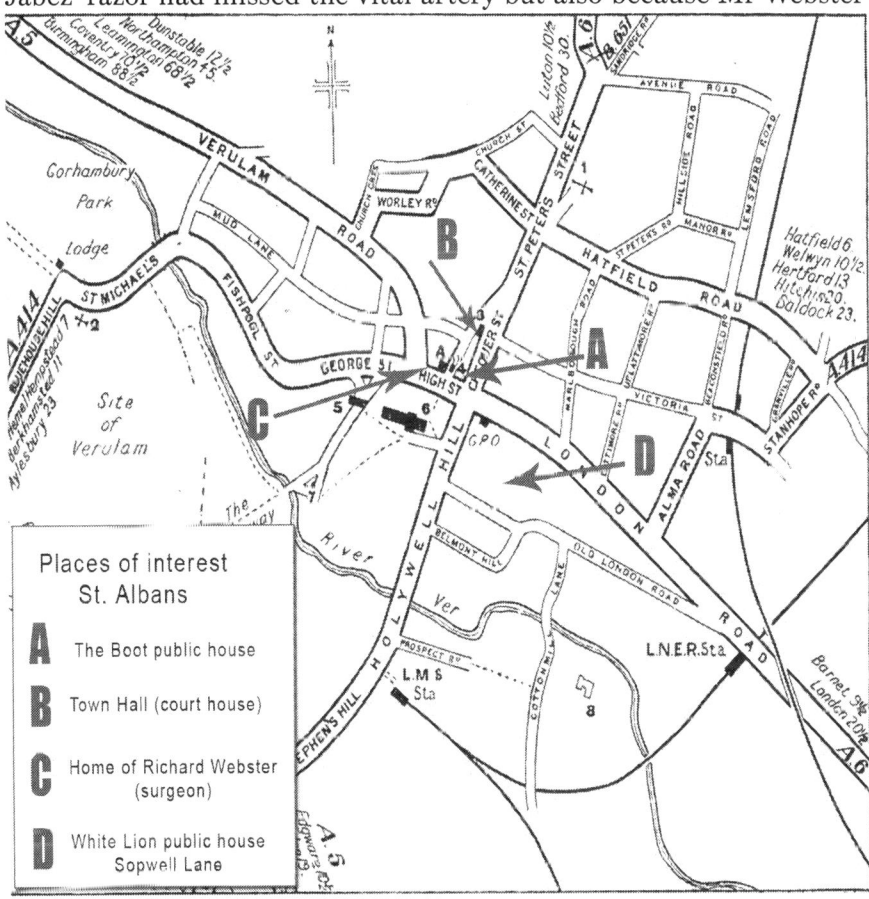

Places of interest
St. Albans

A   The Boot public house

B   Town Hall (court house)

C   Home of Richard Webster (surgeon)

D   White Lion public house Sopwell Lane

was nearby and able to attend the scene. Richard Webster was a retired naval surgeon who had been appointed by Lord Nelson. It would appear that most people who saw Jane after the attack did not think she would survive, in fact the newspapers seemed certain that she would die very soon. Webster, on the other hand, said he had seen much worse injuries and later he was quick to point out that he was confident of her survival from the outset. One can imagine that

Webster had dealt with horrific mutilations during battles at sea and might have persevered giving first aid to Jane where another, less experienced doctor, might have thought her case hopeless.

Although retired from the Navy, Richard Webster was probably still practising as a doctor/surgeon serving the inhabitants of St. Albans; he is listed in the 1841 census as 60 years old, his occupation being 'Surgeon' and another occupant of the house, 25-year-old Robert Robinson listed as 'Assistant'. (The census of 1841 often rounded ages down to the nearest five, so these ages are approximate.) Webster lived in High Street, St. Albans in very close proximity to The Boot.

Jane's evidence

At 12 o'clock Jabez was brought to court. *The Times* (30th October 1841) reported "he walked with a firm step and appeared to command great self possession, considering the awful situation in which he stood."

Jane was led into court accompanied by Mr Webster, the surgeon, Mr Douglas the superintendent of St. Alban's police and a nurse. Her voice was so weak that the town clerk, Mr Blagg was also sworn in so he could relay her words to the rest of the court and the prisoner.

Jane said that she had been living with her sister in Christopher Yard for three or four months. She went on to tell the court that she had known the prisoner as Jabez Kirk and she had met him eight months earlier. The dialogue in The Times report is written as though in response to questioning but there is no indication of what the questions were or who was asking them. She said that during the time she had known Jabez she had been intimate with him and that she had stayed with him at the Boot public house.

The last time she had been to the Boot with Jabez was 9pm on the night of Sunday, 3rd of October and they slept in the same bed. She described how Jabez had asked her, several times, to take off her beads but she told him she never took them off and refused. She said she had no particular reason for refusing. They had not quarrelled and he had never said that he was jealous of anyone. They had nothing to eat or drink during the night until Jabez called for beer and ginger beer early in the morning. She had drank some of the ginger beer and then fell back asleep.

She said she was asleep when she felt a pressure at her neck and had problems breathing. When she came to her senses she put her hands to her throat and 'they went in' to her neck. She was unable to call out or scream and could feel the blood streaming out of her. She looked around and saw Jabez kneeling by her side, his face covered with blood and a razor in his hand. She tried to get up but he pushed her down and a struggle ensued. At one point she managed to free herself and run to the door but Jabez caught her and she fell in the middle of the room and prayed for her life. Jabez threw her back on the bed, held her two hands down and said he would kill her outright. She fought him with her legs and he said he would cut them off if she struggled and she did receive a cut across her leg. When she recounted this part of the struggle the reporter notes that a "universal shudder pervaded the courtroom." A short time later she began to slip into unconsciousness. She went on to say that when she came round her first thought was why he would do this to her. She remembered that Jabez had gone to the door to call for the landlord leaving the razor next to her on the bed. She took this opportunity, weak as she must have been, to slip the razor underneath the mattress because she was afraid he'd come back and cut her again. The next thing she remembered was seeing the policeman, Lacy, in the room and she motioned to him, letting him know where she'd hidden the razor.

Jane went on to give evidence about the razor itself, saying that Jabez had been lent the razor by a solider on *"the Sunday morning before"* and she hadn't seen the razor again until he had cut her with it.

She described Jabez as never having much money and that she never saw any of his money, she expressed surprise as to why he had attacked her and said she would like to know why he had done it. During the whole of Sunday night they had only had some beer and Jabez was quite sober. She described him as a very quiet man who she'd never seen in a 'passion' and that she'd never given him any reason to be angry with her. She said she had been in a very sound sleep when her throat was cut and didn't feel Jabez getting out of bed. She thought that the rest of her injuries must have been inflicted when she was struggling with Jabez.

This was the end of her testimony and it was at this point that Jabez was allowed to question her. He asked that during the time they had been acquainted had she ever seen him tipsy, to which she replied, "No."

The surgeon, Webster took the stand next and gave details of the injuries Jane had suffered. You might want to skip this paragraph if you have a weak stomach or just eaten your breakfast.

He described the main wound was on the left side of her neck, about six inches long extending from about two inches below the lobe of her left ear, straight across the neck to the opposite side of the trachea and being about half an inch deep. It had divided the external jugular vein, one half of the windpipe and some branches of the carotid artery. Beneath this wound there was a vertical cut about two and a half inches long. On Jane's left cheek was another slash that started out being superficial but deepened as it extended backwards, fully dividing the lobe of her ear. She had 15 injuries in all the most serious of the others being to her right hand where her thumb was almost severed by a slash across her palm, severing the tendons. Webster concluded that the necklace of beads, consisting of two or three rows twisted together formed a guard, which protected her neck. They were so entangled that Webster had to cut through them to remove them.

Jabez was then asked for his defence and he only said, "I do not wish to say anything at the present." Questions from the bench were put to him regarding his name and he admitted that his real name was Rainbow, but that he had gone by his mother's maiden name of Kirk since enlisting. He was committed for sentencing at Hertford Assizes.

After the trial Jane was taken to a private room where the magistrates and Webster attempted, over the course of half an hour, to persuade her to go into the workhouse. She refused however and the reporter noted that she "preferred her own miserable home, although Mr. Webster said he would not answer that her life would be safe if she caught cold."

A motive for the attack was never mentioned in court, according to the reports, although more than one newspaper hints at an explanation and are uncharacteristically reticent to share their theories, as quoted here:

> "No motive has been found for the commission of the crime. Several have been hinted at, but as they are entirely the result of imagination, we forbear to mention them."

However *The Times* published on 16th October 1841 added this intriguing sentence at the end of its report:

> "He was jealous of a fellow in the town named Skinner, and there is little doubt that he contemplated his horrid deed some time before he committed it."

Some further investigation reveals that a man named Skinner did indeed feature in Jane's life. Although Mr. Webster, the ex-naval surgeon and Jane's saviour might have been concerned about her future it appears to have been misplaced. In the 1851 census she is still living in Christopher Yard but not with her sister. She is the head of the household, a weaver and has two lodgers Joseph White aged 24 and one Robert Skinner aged 27.

In 1867 Jane married Robert Skinner in St. Albans. In the 1871 census Jane is listed as the wife of Robert Skinner, head, Labourer and living with them is their son, John aged 14 and James Pearce, aged 44, brother (which must be Jane's brother rather than Robert's), also a labourer.

Sentencing

Jabez' final day in court was at Hertford Assizes on 3rd March 1842. He came before the judge Baron Gurney. Gurney was in his 70s and had gained the reputation for being an astute criminal lawyer but a harsh and severe judge.

Jabez was capitally indicted for cutting and wounding Jane Pearse and two other counts to maim and disfigure the prosecutrix and to do her some grievous bodily harm.

The evidence was laid before the jury. They were told that Jane was a female of 'loose character' and she had cohabited with the prisoner for several months. The journalist notes that

> '...the most extraordinary part of the story was that there appeared to be a complete absence of motive on the part of the prisoner for the desperate act he had committed; the girl herself admitting that up to that time he had always been very kind to her and on the day there had not been the slightest quarrel between them" (The Times, 3rd March, 1842)

As the case was summed up Jabez' defence lawyer, Mr C. Jones implored the jury to release his client from the capital indictment for cutting and wounding. They brought in a verdict of guilty for the third count alone, that of grievous bodily harm.

Baron Gurney ordered him to be transported for 15 years.

As the case had progressed several newspapers had linked Jabez' attack on Jane to the notorious Eastcheap murder which had happened just a week earlier. Robert Blakesley had murdered the landlord of a pub and stabbed his estranged wife who was working there. Blakesley had left the scene and gone on the run. Although superficially the two cases were not similar, a police chase to catch Blakesley ended with him being apprehended in Hitchen, just 14 miles away from St. Albans on 27th September. The Hampshire Advertiser commented:

> *"The conduct of the wretch Jabez Kirk affords another illustration of the mania, distemper, infection, contagion or whatever other term medical statisticians choose to adopt, which the commission of a great crime always entails. Whenever one frightful murder is committed the demon chord reverberates in a hundred guilty hearts - in some the impulse overpowers the fear of detection or of punishment, and another life is sacrificed. It has been a common remark, that one murder is sure to be succeeded by a second or third - and the frightful atrocity at St. Albans is but another realisation of its truth. The crime of Kirk was obviously the result of that in Eastcheap, as is proved by the close of the following paragraph.*
>
> *... A sudden fit of jealousy is supposed to have led to the horrible attack on the wretched girl. This murderer in intention and probably in act, purchased on Saturday last off a hawker in St. Albans' Market, a broad sheet, illustrated with cuts, containing an account of the Eastcheap murder. This he had in his pocket at the time he attempted to commit a similar crime; and after he was conveyed to the lock-up employed himself in repeatedly reading it."*

Hampshire Advertiser & Salisbury Guardian (Southampton, England), Saturday, October 09, 1841; Issue 951. *19th Century British Library Newspapers: Part II.*

Although the newspapers contain a lot of information about the attack on Jane Pearse there are also more questions than answers.

There would seem to be no doubt that Jabez committed the crime. He admitted to it immediately and there was no implication that there was anybody else involved. So what was the motivation? If it was jealousy as one or two newspapers implied and the fact that Jane went on to live with and then marry Skinner seems to point in that direction then why wasn't that mentioned in court? In fact Jane denied that she had ever done anything to make Jabez jealous. Was she trying to protect what was left of her reputation? Being intimate with one man was bad enough but two?

Why would a girl only have good things to say about a man who had cut her throat while she slept? Fear that he may come after her and finish the job? It's a possibility, but she would have known that the minimum sentence would see him safely transported to the other side of the world and if she had been more forceful with her evidence it's very likely he would have been sentenced to death. Was she trying to spare his life? From the reported accounts she doesn't even appear to be angry just puzzled. It's a possibility that there was much pressure on her to appear in court after several adjournments, maybe she had been given some type of medication and that affected her ability to communicate.

Why would a jury cast aside the capital indictment and spare Jabez' life? In essence they were agreeing that this was not a cold and calculating murder attempt but rather Jabez committed this act while he was suffering under the "paroxysm of temporary madness". Yet, here we have a man who cut his lover's throat as she lay sleeping. There had been no raised voices, no arguments and no mention of him being jealous of another man. She lay asleep and he quietly took a razor to her throat, the only struggle being when she woke up to discover what he was doing. If ever there was an example of a cold-blooded crime, surely this was it.

Then there is Jabez' rather bizarre defence. In those days it was acceptable for the defendant to question witnesses. He chose to ask only two questions one to Jane about being tipsy and one to Foxall the landlord of The Boot. Both newspaper reports are a little unclear with the wording of this question but Jabez seems to either be disputing how many times he called out "Murder!" when Foxall saw him at the top of the stairs or questioning his certainty about the identity of the person he saw at the top of the stairs or indeed who actually called out "Murder!".

The Morning Chronicle (October 9th 1841) quotes "Cross-examined by the prisoner [Foxall replies] I am quite sure, on you coming to the top of the stair, you only called 'murder' twice.

Then the magistrate cross-examines Foxall who replies, "I saw the prisoner at the time he called out 'murder'. I was standing looking at him."

So here is a man literally fighting for his life and his questions do not appear to be at all pertinent unless there was additional information revealed in court that was not reported. The tipsy question seems irrelevant when both Jane and Foxall had already given evidence suggesting that either they had never seen him drunk or that drink wasn't a problem to him. According to all the witnesses Jabez was a sober man. On 24th July 1842 when he arrived in Van Diemen's Land, his convict record was filled in with details of his age, appearance and crime, including this quote from the prisoner himself:

"Stated this offence. Stabbing my sweetheart in the throat with a razor in a Public House. I had been drinking several days."

Was this an easy answer to give an official who was looking for an explanation? Alternatively maybe this was closer to the truth and the witnesses who said otherwise were trying to save his life? Could they have been persuaded or even bribed? There is no mention of Jabez' father Joseph so we have no way of knowing if he attended the trial or even knew about his son's crime, although it was featured in the local Coventry newspaper so it seems likely that he would have been aware.

It was commented on in several newspapers that Jabez came from a 'respectable family' or that he had 'good connections'. Joseph, being a lawyer's clerk would also have had contacts in the legal profession, maybe he called in some favours? The truth is that it is unlikely that we'll ever find the answers to these questions.

I'd never heard the story of Jabez until I chanced upon the article in the archives and the likelihood is that it was hushed up in the family. I was sent a copy of a family tree based on research completed by 'Aunt Alice' who I believe to have been Amy Alice Watts Rainbow (1865-1942). On the tree are all the birth and death dates of Joseph's children, included Jabez'. Someone in England must have had contact with Tasmania because his death does not appear in UK records.

Was Jabez, a psychopath or a troubled young man, a victim of jealousy and alcohol? Whatever his mental state or motivation he is our very own black sheep.

The Journey

After being sentenced at St. Albans, Jabez was sent to a hulk to await for his ship to Van Diemen's Land. On his convict record in the Hobart archives it records that his behaviour on board the hulk was 'Good'.

Regular prisons in Victorian England were horrendously overcrowded. As the industrial revolution took hold in earnest and country people flocked to the towns for work the ensuing poverty, poor housing and crowded conditions led to a sharp increase in the crime rate. Wealthy town residents, fearing that they were being overrun and determined to stamp out this rising tide of criminal activity imposed ever more draconian sentences. Although Jabez had committed a serious and violent crime he would have been sharing his confinement with men, women and even children who had engaged in relatively minor criminal offences, at least from a modern perspective. As the prisons spilled over, convicts awaiting transportation were housed in hulks. These were old war ships that were no longer seaworthy but pressed into service to contain hundreds of convicts caged and chained in the hold. Sails, masts and guns were removed leaving the hull remaining. In 1841 three thousand prisoners were imprisoned in nine hulks moored off the English coast at Deptford, Portsmouth and at the Royal Arsenal docks at Woolwich. Weeks, months and even years were spent on these containers awaiting transportation.

Several hulks were moored in the Thames at Woolwich and records show that Jabez was imprisoned on the Justitia. One account by a prisoner who was sent to the Justitia approximately 18 months before Jabez describes arriving from gaol with fellow prisoners. Before going aboard they were stripped and scrubbed with soap and a stiff brush until blood ran, their hair was clipped close to their heads and they put on their 'magpie' uniforms. Washing and the provision of clean clothes was an attempt to stop the spread of disease that often ran riot through the confined quarters of the hulk. Many of the prisoners would still be wearing the clothes they were convicted in, complete with lice. The so-called magpie uniform had one side blue or black and the other side yellow making any escapee conspicuous to local residents. The prisoners were then taken to the blacksmith where iron rings were riveted around their ankles. Eight links connected the ankle rings with a ring in the centre where a strap was connected, the other end attached to the their belts. This stopped the chain from dragging on the floor. They were issued with a number, no names were used and during the day gangs of prisoners would be taken off the hulks to work in the naval dockyard. This was hard labour and involved building fortifications and manufacturing ammunition.

At Woolwich, the hulks were usually moored on the south shore of the Thames, but if there was unrest amongst the prisoners the boat would be moved to the north shore. Prisoners making an escape attempt were more likely to try when it was moored near populated Woolwich rather than the Essex marshes, which had a reputation for harbouring disease, and were rumoured to be the cause of mysterious deaths. Conditions on the hulk were generally grim with hundreds of men living cheek by jowl in overcrowded and unsanitary circumstances. Food was often mouldy or maggoty and when there was an attempt to improve conditions by supplying wholesome food there was a public backlash with outcries that prisoners were having it too easy.

Jabez eventually travelled to Van Diemen's Land on the prison ship, The Susan, which set sail from Plymouth on 24th April 1842 and arrived in Van Diemen's Land on 25th July. The ship carried 299 male convicts of which 297 survived the journey. Transportation to Van Diemen's Land officially ended in 1853 and was finally ended completely in 1857. Conditions on board the ships were grim, albeit they had improved from earlier voyages. There appears to be very little information regarding Jabez' journey aboard The Susan but a ship's surgeon, Colin A. Browning wrote an account of his work on board convict ships including The Earl Grey, which sailed from Plymouth to Van Diemen's Land less than a year after The Susan. We might assume that conditions were similar.

The three month voyage to the southern hemisphere appears to have been grasped, in the more enlightened 1840s, as an opportunity to educate and reform rather than merely chain and contain the prisoners. A great emphasis seems to have been placed on religious education and Browning, writing about a voyage on the convict ship Theresa, believed that practical Christianity was an alternative to corporal punishment and reports that 156 out of 220 prisoners turned to the Lord during the voyage and because of this no lashings were administered and no prisoner had to be put under guard. From a twenty first century perspective, we know that those who are subjected to claustrophobic and restricted living conditions can be greatly influenced by the authority figures controlling their lives, so this high proportion of converts is probably not surprising, particularly given the alternative.

Browning describes The Earl Grey dropping anchor at Woolwich to pick up prisoners for transportation. The prisoners were brought up to the hulk deck and listened to various addresses from clergy and captain urging them to grasp the opportunities before them and the atmosphere seemed to be one of anticipation. The embarkation of the men to the Earl Grey went according to plan although Browning was perturbed that a petty officer had allowed one of the men to play his violin while they waited for the Earl Grey to come alongside the hulk. Brown thought this 'highly indecorous' and likely to have an "injurious influence" on the minds of the prisoners. Browning thought the occasion desired the utmost solemnity.

Shortly after being allocated their quarters the prisoners were assembled on the quarterdeck in order to ascertain their literacy. It would seem that Jabez may have been among the minority of prisoners who could both read and write. On Browning's ship less than a quarter had this level of education. The prisoners were then divided up into 'schools' according to ability, each with their own teacher and daily instruction took place. Browning commented that the hum of industry coming from the schools is more attractive than the finest music and that the pupils, as well as learning to read, are acquiring useful information as much of the texts used are 'valuable little works published by the Tract Society.' (The Tract Society was the original name of a publisher of Christian literature intended initially for evangelism, and including literature aimed at children, women, and the poor.)

Prisoners were assembled twice a day for 'church' at 10am and again at 2pm where they read bible stories and sang hymns. Browning expounds,

> "It is difficult to imagine and spectacle more impressive than that of 264 outcasts, consigned by the violated laws of their country to all the horrors of transportation, closely seated on the quarterdeck of a transport, under sail to a remote quarter of the earth, with scarcely a hope ever again to tread their native shores, or to behold, in the flesh, those who are dearest to their hearts, and the ship's company, the soldiers, their wives and children, all in their sabbath day costumes, arranged in their proper places on deck, all seriously engaged in solemn worship of the Most High."

Browning saw himself as very much doing the Lord's work in transporting these prisoners from hell to heaven, from Satan to God and there is no way of knowing if religious fervour was as motivating for the crew of Jabez' ship, The Susan. The frequent services on board The Earl Grey must have been a welcome break after the hard labour of the naval dockyard and before the unknown in Van Diemen's Land. No surprise then that the prisoners embraced their new faith with enthusiasm and even happiness. We might have images of convict ships that were full of desperately miserable convicts who would have given anything to remain in England but this doesn't appear to be the case. Browning describes how one man became sick shortly after leaving Woolwich and Browning applied for his debarkation at Plymouth, afraid for his health on such a long voyage. Rather than being relieved the man sent Browning a note begging to be allowed to stay onboard and assuring him that he would be better once they arrived at milder climates. Browning relented, the man remained on board and his health had improved by the time the ship reached Madeira. Browning records that this man became one his best scripture teachers a 'true child of God'.

Various positions were assigned to prisoners and these were allocated after referring to conduct reports from both the gaol and hulk where they had previously been incarcerated. A librarian was appointed to look after the 'schoolbooks', distribute them to the teachers and maintain them, repairing the bindings when necessary. A barber was appointed who shaved the prisoners twice a week, the razors being returned to the petty officers after each session for safekeeping! Clothes were washed regularly and bedding brought up to the deck to be aired. Each afternoon, lessons other than scripture studies were permitted and a 'popular lecture could be delivered, in a colloquial style', with subjects such as geography, philosophy or astronomy or anything that would interest, *enlighten and improve the minds of the hearers.*' Exercise on board ship consisted of small groups of prisoners marching around the deck to music for fifteen to twenty minutes. After 14 days at sea prisoners were given a daily allowance of wine, limejuice and sugar to prevent scurvy, the disease caused by a lack of vitamin C in the absence of fresh fruits and vegetables in the diet.

After three months at sea The Earl Grey finally docked at Hobart Town, Van Diemen's Land. An army officer who was also a justice of the peace came aboard to join the last service on the deck of the ship. He gave a talk to the prisoners describing the temptations that they would face in their new country. He urged them not to drink but instead to join the Temperance Society. At the end of the service the prisoners presented Browning with a letter thanking him for his spiritual guidance throughout the voyage.

Browning reports that at 3am on the morning of January 20th 1843 boats came alongside the Earl Grey and the debarkation of the prisoners was conducted in a speedy, orderly fashion in perfect silence.

On land, Sir John Franklin, Lieutenant-Governor of Van Deimen's Land, addressed the prisoners. He was to be removed from office later that year because his humane attitudes and attempts to reform the penal colony had angered local civil servants. On this occasion he spoke positively about the appearance of the prisoners and their behaviour during their time aboard the Earl Grey.

In the second part of Browning's book he writes about how prisoners fared once they had left the confines of the transportation ship. He was particularly concerned as to how his 'own' prisoners had coped in their new surroundings. He points out the difficulties of obtaining this information, or at least accurate information as he casts some doubt on the police and official reports that he had been able to obtain.

Browning is able to gather some information directly from prisoners. One writes him a letter describing the harsh conditions in Van Diemen's Land. He describes being chained to other prisoners, a few from his ship along with some 'old hands' and marching the fifty miles to establish a new station in the bush. Several months on a ship with a limited chance for exercise had made the newcomers weak and they found it difficult to walk under these circumstances but no allowance was made. The writer expressed his disappointment at the coarse and vulgar language of the established convicts and commented that the system appeared to be one that hardened men rather than reformed them. He went on to describe the different forms of punishment administered for various offences, with one prisoner being appointed to be the official flagellator. A 'triangle' was erected and 'the cat' used on a regular basis. The triangle was a tripod of wooden beams where the offender was suspended by the wrists, stripped to the waist and one or two floggers would administer lashes either with a single whip or the dreaded 'cat o'nine tails', a whip made up of nine strands of knotted cotton cord made to inflict the most pain and damage.

Life in Van Diemen's Land

Tasmania, formerly known as Van Diemen's Land, is a state of Australia located 150 miles to the south and separated by the Bass Strait. It is an area of 26,000 square miles making it the 26th biggest island in the world and in 2008 it had a population of 500,000. It is estimated that Tasmania was separated from mainland Australia about 10,000 years ago by rising sea levels.

The island of Tasmania was 'discovered' by Dutch explorer, Abel Tasman in 1642 and was home, at that time, to approximately 9 indigenous aboriginal tribes numbering about 5,000 to 10,000. By the time Jabez was transported to the island in 1843, the native population had been largely decimated by both disease and persecution and apart from a small population of white, free settlers VDL had become, for the most part, a convict settlement. Between 1803 and 1853 approximately 75,000 prisoners were transported from the UK to begin their new lives in the penal colony.

Although Australia had been a difficult country for new settlers because of the harsh environment and lack of native game, Van Diemen's Land was a very different experience. Warm and sheltered, it proved to be an environmental paradise even compared to Britain. It had a temperate climate, an abundance of game, dependable rainfall and open grasslands. Moreover at the time of the first settlers, in 1803 there was no native dog population; Van Diemen's Land was one of the few places on earth where dogs were unknown. This meant that the local game, such as kangaroos and wallabies were unprepared for the settlers' hunting dogs. In his book *Van Diemen's Land*, James Boyce states that the health of the population was far superior to that of the working class in England.

John West, in his book, The History of Tasmania, written in 1852, states that in the 1840s the convicts in Van Diemen's Land outnumbered the settlers' children; that they amounted to nearly double the adult free population and that only one fifth were female. Conditions for prisoners were regarded to be amongst the harshest in the world. In 1832 the governor of New South Wales and VDL issued Regulations for Penal Settlements, which were only partially acted upon.

It was believed that a lack of honesty and avoidance of hard work was what brought most of them to crime, therefore prisoners would be required to work at something that was simple, easy to understand and had a degree of uniformity which they could not evade. When the public works department didn't require their labour they were to be employed on the land using a hoe or spade. No plough and no working cattle were allowed.

In order to afford effective supervision, the men had to be spaced at equal distances apart, we might assume that was to prevent them communicating with each other.

The convicts were to be employed at hard labour from sunrise to sunset with one hour allowed for breakfast and one hour for dinner during the winter and two hours for dinner during the summer.

As a reward and encouragement for good conduct the prisoners were divided into two classes, first and second. Prisoners were not eligible to be admitted to first class unless they had served two years if their sentence was seven years, four years if their sentence was fourteen, and six years if they had been given life. Once a prisoner was admitted to the first class group he was allowed one ounce of tobacco a week in addition to his usual rations, he was given lighter duties and was also eligible to be assigned as a servant to an officer, entrusted with charge of live stock and other trustworthy occupations. He was also eligible to be chosen to act as a constable or overseer.

From his prison record it would appear that Jabez was a compliant convict. He was initially stationed at Impression Bay (now Preyimbula), a probation station about 11 miles (18K) from the notorious Port Arthur penitentiary. The Impression Bay station was opened in 1841 when the new probation system was established. This less brutal scheme, allowed for convict gangs to work on public works, such as roads and eventually a prisoner was able to earn a Ticket of Leave, which gave him permission to 'employ himself for his own benefit' and to acquire property with certain conditions. He would be required to reside within a specified district and he must attend church on a weekly basis. The governor was allowed to rescind the ticket at any time and the individual would revert to becoming a prisoner again. This was an experimental system that ultimately failed.

The theory behind the idea was that punishment and reform could be achieved by a combination of confinement, hard labour and education. Punishment became less severe the longer good behaviour continued, leading to the Ticket of Leave and eventually a pardon. However, the system was overwhelmed and ultimately failed because of the large numbers involved, poor management, inadequate funding and the economic depression of 1846. Moreover, there was little employment for the ticket of leave holders and they were left to languish at the probation stations employed in public works while they waited for an employer to take them on.

Jabez appears to have been relatively fortunate to have been transported when he did. The less harsh probation system had just been established and the more benign governorship of Franklin was firmly in place when he arrived at Impression Bay. Although this didn't last for his full sentence it was in operation for arguably the toughest period, the first year.

Comments were entered at regular intervals on Jabez' convict record and these were either 'Quiet', 'Orderly' or 'Good'. There were no other crimes noted and he appears to have been a model prisoner. On 24th July 1848 he was released from the 1st stage of his probation and his Ticket of Leave granted on 1st August 1848. He was recommended to apply for a conditional pardon in six months on 24th February 1849 and was granted it on 15th October 1850.

Women were in short supply on Van Diemen's Land, so much so that in 1831 the British Government used the proceeds from the sales of land to encourage women between the ages of 15 and 30 to emigrate

Chasing Rainbows

with an allowance of £8, which was about half the cost of the voyage. Women were wanted on Van Diemen's Land, not only to work 'in service' for the free settlers but also to marry the male convicts. It was believed that being married and having a family would have a calming influence on the men and neutralise the brutal and often violent all male community. There were also accusations that 'unnatural practices' were being practised and although homosexuality would not be surprising in an all male environment it may be that Victorian attitudes may have contributed to a degree of exaggeration of this 'problem'.

Chasing Rainbows

The Tasmanians

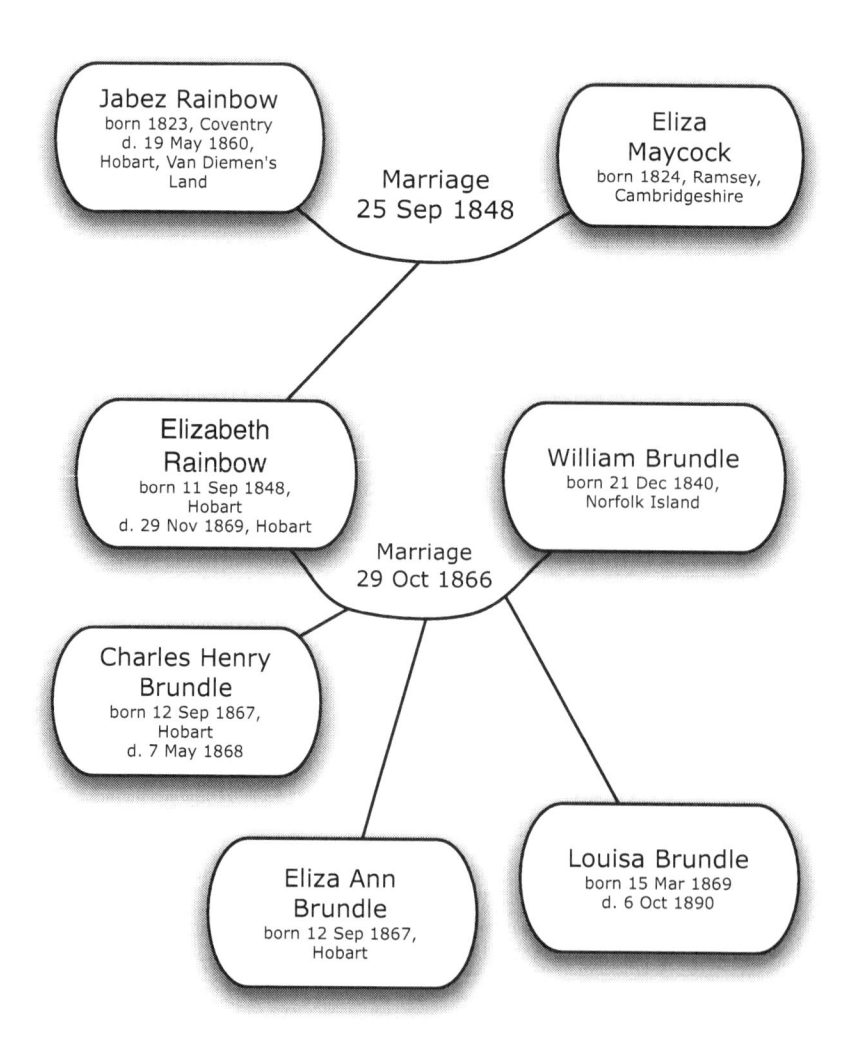

- **Jabez Rainbow** — born 1823, Coventry; d. 19 May 1860, Hobart, Van Diemen's Land
- **Eliza Maycock** — born 1824, Ramsey, Cambridgeshire
- Marriage 25 Sep 1848

- **Elizabeth Rainbow** — born 11 Sep 1848, Hobart; d. 29 Nov 1869, Hobart
- **William Brundle** — born 21 Dec 1840, Norfolk Island
- Marriage 29 Oct 1866

- **Charles Henry Brundle** — born 12 Sep 1867, Hobart; d. 7 May 1868
- **Eliza Ann Brundle** — born 12 Sep 1867, Hobart
- **Louisa Brundle** — born 15 Mar 1869; d. 6 Oct 1890

Married Life

Six weeks after he was granted his Ticket of Leave, on 25th September 1848 Jabez married Eliza Maycock. She was 23 years old, a year younger than Jabez and also a convict. She had given birth to their daughter, just two weeks earlier on 11th September. The marriage approval was published in the Hobart Colonial Times in accordance with an Act of Parliament and reads:

> "Jabez Rainbow, T.L., Susan 2, and Eliza Maycock, Sea Queen, in private service, both residing in Hobart Town."

Eliza Maycock

Eliza had been born in Ramsey, Cambridgeshire in 1824 and had arrived in Van Damien's Land in 1846. She had been been transported for setting her employer's hay barn on fire.

In the Essex Standard of Friday 16th January 1846 there was a report of a serious fire at the homestead of Mr Henry Bridgfoot who owned a farm about five miles outside Ramsey. It started about 7.30pm and could be seen from miles around. Fire engines and neighbours rushed to the scene and helped to put out the fire, which was finally damped down around 1am. It was stated that Mrs Bridgfoot was suffering ill health and suffered convulsions as their farm burned and their eight children had to be removed to a neighbour's *'crying and screaming in the most distressing manner'*. Such was the seriousness of the fire that local residents called for any enquiry and the local coroner summoned a jury to hear the case.

The inhabitants of the farm were interviewed at great length, including the Bridgfoots and four servants, two boys, Eliza Maycock and Jane Taylor. There appeared to be some inconsistencies with Eliza's evidence which included the fact that she'd mentioned to Mrs

Bridgfoot that she'd had a dream two or three weeks earlier that two strange men had set fire to the Bridgfoot's farm. However, guilt could not be determined at that time and the case was adjourned. Eliza was sent to a neighbouring house to be kept away from other witnesses and Jane Taylor observed that on her way home she appeared *'low-spirited and half-mad'*. When she eventually met up with Mr Bridgfoot he questioned her about the discrepancies in her evidence. She burst into tears and confessed. The police were called and she was placed in custody awaiting trial.

> *"At Huntington assizes on Friday, Eliza Maycock, a stout surly looking girl of twenty one was convicted of maliciously setting fire to three stacks of corn, hay, etc."*

from The Chronicle on 24th March 1846

Eliza was sentenced to 15 years and transported, along with 169 other females to Van Diemen's Land. The Sea Queen left Woolwich on 12th May 1846 and arrived on 29th August of the same year.

Eliza's convict record describes her as a housemaid, 5 foot 5 inches tall, aged 20 with a dark complexion, black hair and eyes, 'small and double' chin and missing a front tooth. Her religion is given as Roman Catholic and she can read but not write.

Most female convicts were sent to one of several female 'factories'. There were four in Van Diemen's Land, The Cascades, Launceston, Ross and George Town. Conditions there were so bad that women were sometimes kept on board their convict ship until suitable employment could be found for them rather than having to endure the crowded and chaotic conditions at the 'factory'. After searching the databases for the factories I can find no record of Eliza, although this doesn't mean she wasn't there as the databases are a work in progress. Maybe she was one of the 'lucky' ones who went straight to employment, working for a settler. Her convict record notes that she is 'good, industrious and useful' and her probationary period only lasted for 6 months.

Eliza was granted her Ticket of Leave in January 1853 and her Conditional Pardon on 19th December 1854.

It would appear then that Eliza was working in private service in Hobart at the time of her marriage to Jabez. One wonders what the reaction of her employer was to her becoming pregnant and the fact that they didn't marry until two weeks after the baby was born. I know very little about their lives after this, except that at the time of their daughter's birth Jabez was a porter and at some point later took up employment as a 'letter carrier' for the Post Office in Hobart.

In 1928 the Hobart Mercury published an article taken from 'Wood's Tasmanian Almanack for 1856,' one of a series looking back at old Hobart. The article's focus was on Hobart postmen and gives us a good idea of what Jabez's daily routine would have been. There were three deliveries a day at 9am, 1pm and 4pm starting from the General Post Office. Every evening (except Sunday) the men would patrol their beats between 5pm and 6pm ringing a bell in order to collect post and newspapers that residents wanted delivering. The post had to be prepaid with stamps and the letter carrier could collect one penny for every letter and a ha'penny for every newspaper, which was his to keep.

Postmen were expected to wear their livery at all times when on duty and the public were instructed to place their letter into the carrier's bag themselves. At the end of the article there is a list of postmen employed at that time: Joseph Brown, James Walker, Daniel Lillingtstone, Jabez Rainbow, Stephen Swaysland and John Walley and details of their renumeration, '5/6 per diem each.' This was 5 shillings and 6 pence in the pre-decimal currency of the time. In the 1850s this would have been about the equivalent of £16 per day in today's currency and was about the average for a craftsman working in the building trade. Given the opportunity to earn extra with collections this would seem to be a relatively well-paid job.

THE TICKNER MURDER MYSTERY

Jabez died, aged 37. His obituary in the Hobart Town Advertiser of May 22nd 1860 leaves us with another puzzle. It says that the well-known letter carrier died in the general hospital after suffering from delirium. For several weeks he had been showing signs of 'mental aberration' and had been allowed leave from his work at the Post Office. It continued; a few weeks earlier a rumour had been spread about the alleged murderer of the Tickners who it was said was 'a highly respectable resident of Hobart Town'. However this rumour, it appeared, had been traced back to Jabez who was suffering from delirium at the time. It concludes by saying he will be missed by his *'large family'* and that he had worked at the Post Office for some years.

After a little research I found several newspaper articles reporting the Tickner double murder case.

George and Mary Tickner lived in Adelaide Street, Hobart. George was a dealer in hay and had recently purchased a cottage in Adelaide Street at the upper end of Davey Street. He was also an 'old man' of about 60 and Mary was at least a decade younger than him. Tickner was known to be well off, often with rolls of notes on him. Although they lived as man and wife, George Tickner and Mary Calvert were not legally married and were known to have loud, violent, alcohol fuelled rows.

On Saturday 18th February 1860 at 5am a labourer called John Plummer was passing the cottage when he saw George Tickner, wearing only a shirt, lying in the yard. He was dying from severe head wounds. Plummer went into the house and found Mary, also dying from dreadful wounds to the skull. Plummer called for the doctor but George died before he arrived and Mary an hour later.

A jury was summoned for the inquest to be held to determine the cause of death. A policeman gave evidence that he had passed the house at 4.30am and there was nothing untoward that aroused his suspicions.

The jury were taken out to look at the house and the injuries were described to them. Although the motive may have been robbery the police had found packs of sovereigns hidden in an outhouse, the bedroom didn't appear to have been disturbed and George still had his gold watch. The cottage was within a few yards of neighbours but nobody had heard any disturbance. No weapon or footsteps were discovered.

An addendum to the report in *The Hobart Town Daily Mercury* stated that the man John Plummer was in custody alongside a woodman, Thomas Harrison, both suspected of the murder.

I haven't been able to find any details of a trial for these men but on 25th February The Hobart newspaper published another report of the murder and ended with the closing sentence that a 'man named Charles Williams was apprehended yesterday morning on suspicion of these fearful murders.' Again, no more information about any trial or conviction but then on Monday 14th May 1860 another small article appeared in *The Hobart Town Daily Mercury* saying that a man named Owen Callaghan, a shoemaker, was taken into custody whilst trying to make his escape into the bush. Callaghan along with his wife, Mary had been charged with the murders of the Tickners in February.

Yet again I can find no evidence of a court case involving Owen and Mary Callaghan but jumping forward a few years the case comes up again. On the 14th March 1867 *The Hobart Mercury* reports on the proceedings that took place in New Zealand against Jas. Baxter alias Allan McGregor. He was on remand on the charge of murdering Mr and Mrs Tickner in Hobart. Apparently at some point Baxter had confessed to the murder but in court was denying all knowledge of committing the crime. The Hobart detectives applied for the discharge of the prisoner, presumably intending to take him back to Hobart. The magistrate discharged the accused and ordered that he should be taken to hospital immediately as he appeared to be suffering from a serious illness. No more information is available until two years later, 20th May 1869. *The Hobart Mercury* published a letter from a Horace Browne who said that although James Baxter had confessed to the Tickner murders he knew that it was impossible for him to have committed the crime. He asserts that Baxter was under his 'direct observation' from 3am until 6.30am that day, so it could not possibly have been him. He concludes that it was the influence of drink that made Baxter talk about murders and robberies. Beneath this letter the editor notes that the police are fully aware that the man Baxter is not the murderer of the Tickners. He confessed the crime in New Zealand some months ago; Detective Vickers was sent from Hobart and Baxter was discharged.

At the time of writing I can find no additional information about this crime and no indication to which 'highly respectable' resident Jabez referred when he levelled his allegedly delirium fuelled accusation.

After the murders were committed and in the space of a few weeks at least five people had been accused and presumably discarded as suspects. So although, initially, Jabez' claim that a highly respected member of the community committed the murders set off my conspiracy theory alarms it may be more understandable given that this crime, with no obvious perpetrators, would have created quite a stir in a relatively small town (population approximately 60,000). We might imagine that speculation was rife and that someone like Jabez having access to many people through his employment and already suffering with some kind of mental illness might get enmeshed in the drama. On the other hand if Jabez really was mentally ill why lend any credence to the story by publishing it in his obituary. Perhaps this was an attempt to discredit a story that was beginning to develop in credibility?

After Jabez' death I can find no other information about Eliza except that thirteen years later, in 1873 she married a man called William Whitbread.

The Brundles - the next generation?

I thought I had the next generation of Tasmanian Rainbows all figured out, but as is often the case with family history, a new piece of information emerges and throws everything up in the air.

When I did the initial research for Jabez and his family around 2004 I was helped by a researcher in Tasmania that I 'met' in a convict research online chat group. She kindly offered to find Jabez' records in the Hobart archives, photocopy them and send them via snail mail. At this time none of the records were online and this was the only practical way to get hold of the information.

I remember the day when the fat, brown envelope arrived from Tasmania and the excitement of pulling out A3 copies of not only Jabez' convict record, but the record of his marriage to Eliza, the birth of his daughter, his death, Eliza's second marriage, his daughter's marriage, the birth of his grandchildren, etc. I had two further generations ready-made. Or so I thought.

Here's the problem. Let me lay out the evidence, both for and against and you can decide:

The researcher in Tasmania told me that Jabez and Eliza had a baby girl on September 11th 1848 and sent me further details of this child's life. Elizabeth grew up to marry William Brundle and they had three children including Louisa Brundle. Both Elizabeth and later, her daughter Louisa, coincidentally and tragically, died at the age of 21.

Now to backtrack a little; during the time I've researched the Tasmanian Rainbows I've had a problem concerning confusion with another Rainbow branch. A certain Joseph Rainbow, who was born in Adderbury Oxford on 20th October 1807, was transported to VDL for horse stealing in 1829, 13 years earlier than Jabez. He went on to marry Elizabeth Bennett and had a large family. Because Jabez' father was also called Joseph and Rainbow being a reasonably uncommon name another researcher must have jumped to the conclusion that the horse stealing Joseph must have been Jabez' father. The most compelling reasons that the Tasmanian Joseph is not Jabez' father is:

- Joseph Rainbow, the real father of Jabez appeared on every UK census living in Coventry, up until his death in 1859.
- Joseph is buried at London Road Cemetery, Coventry

The link between Jabez Rainbow and his father, the lawyer's clerk in Coventry is well documented and the erroneous information seems to be the result of one researcher mistakenly linking two Rainbows, posting the information on the internet and it spread out from there.

Back to Jabez and Eliza in Van Diemen's Land and the birth of their daughter, Elizabeth, in 1848. Whilst double-checking records in preparation for writing this book I came across Births, Deaths and Marriage records that are now available online from the Archives Office of Tasmania. I searched for Rainbows in births and found four Elizabeth Rainbows. The ones born in 1814 and 1871 are way out of date range, leaving two that were both born in 1847, just a year out from 'our' Elizabeth. One only included details of her marriage in 1867 to a James Gunton with no details of parents. The last record gives Elizabeth's parents as Joseph (horse thief) Rainbow and Elizabeth Bennett, with a marriage to William Brundle and three children, Eliza Ann, Charles Henry and Louisa Brundle.

Now I was confused. It was 'our' Elizabeth that married William Brundle. Why was she linked to our old friend, Joseph (horse thief) Rainbow? I realised that I had a photocopy of Jabez and Eliza's child's birth record and checking found, to my surprise, that at the time of the registration the child had not been named. My first thought was that maybe the baby died at birth or shortly afterwards, but the registration took place almost 6 weeks after the birth so that was unlikely. Although it's possible that they hadn't decided on a name for their child after 6 weeks, looking again at the photocopied page of the register I could see that there were 5 other birth registrations written in for that day, in Hobart on 16th October 1848, and none of the babies had been given names. This would point to some sort of failure on the part of the registrar rather than parents who couldn't make up their minds.

So we have an unnamed female Rainbow born on 11th September 1848, in Hobart to Jabez and Eliza for certain, but what was her name and what happened to her?

Going back to the archives I found an unnamed female Rainbow born in 1848 but with no further details. ***This was the only female Rainbow in the archives born in 1848 in Hobart.***

I checked the wedding record of William Brundle and Elizabeth Rainbow and they married on 29th October 1866 and Elizabeth's age was given as 18. This would fit our girl, as she would have just turned 18 in October 1866. Joseph Rainbow's Elizabeth would have been 19 years old on that date. Unfortunately it wasn't until several decades later that the names of fathers were required information on wedding records - this would have answered the question.

Given the evidence my feeling is that Jabez and Eliza's daughter was the Elizabeth that married William Brundle and the other Elizabeth, Joseph Rainbow's daughter, was the one that married James Gunton. Somehow the records of Elizabeth Rainbows have been replicated. I wondered how this could happened when these were official archives until I read the disclaimer: "The family links in the database have not been made by the Archives Office and we are not therefore able to guarantee their accuracy."

So that's my position. At the moment I can't find further records to verify this but I'll include the information that I have about Elizabeth and the Brundles, as I believe that the Elizabeth Rainbow who married William Brundle **is** the daughter of Jabez and Eliza Rainbow.

Dying Young

Elizabeth Rainbow was born in Hobart on 11th September 1848. I know very little about her life except that she married William Brundle when she was 18 and had three children before her death at the age of 21. William was stated to be a 'Tradesman' on their wedding day on 29th October 1866 and he was variously described as a shoemaker (on Elizabeth's death certificate), bootmaker (on his daughter Louisa's birth record) and a tobacconist later in his life.

Their children, twins Charles Henry and Eliza Ann Brundle were born on 12th September 1867, but Charles died when he was 9 months old on 7th May 1868. On 15th March 1869 their second daughter, Louisa Brundle was born. The two girls were left motherless when Elizabeth died less than 9 months later. The cause of death was 'Asthemia caused by fright.' The term asthemia is not widely used in medicine today. It means weakness, lack of energy and strength. I've scoured the newspapers of the period and there is no mention of her death, not even a family announcement and the Tasmanian archives have no record of an inquest. This would be mysterious in itself but there was more to come.

I haven't found a record of William remarrying or have any idea of what help he may have had with raising two babies on his own and presumably working full time as a shoemaker. The girls survived childhood and it is very likely that Eliza Ann married but there are at least two records of marriages for an Eliza Ann Brundle of Hobart and at the time of writing I haven't pinned 'our' Eliza down. One marriage is to a man called Howard Hayton of Hobart and the other is to a man in New Zealand. More research required! Her younger sister, Louisa, however, we do know a little more about.

'A death under rather singular circumstances'

Louisa presents us with a different kind of mystery. At the age of 21, Louisa Brundle was a 'tobacconist's daughter', living with her father in Elizabeth Street, Hobart. On 6th October 1890 she died from an unknown cause whilst on a carriage drive with Alderman Thomas Alcott, a butcher, councillor and much older, married man.

The sudden death of a young and ostensibly healthy young woman was the subject of an inquest, which was reported extensively in the local newspapers.

Wednesday 8th October 1890

William Brundle, Louisa's father gave evidence at the inquest and stated that Louisa was his daughter and the last time he had seen her alive was at 1.30pm on Monday 6th and that she appeared to be in good health. He thought she had been at work in the afternoon but did not know where she was after 1.30pm until Alderman Amott and Dr Hardy informed him she had died. He said she had never been ill.

Alderman Thomas Amott was called to give evidence and he said that he knew Louisa and had seen her on Monday afternoon at about five minutes to three. He had gone to meet her in the Domain[5], between the cricket ground and the quarry after having received a note saying she wanted to see him without fail. He rode out in a trap and said Louisa was pacing up and down the road when he saw her. She appeared to have been crying and was excited. When he asked her what was wrong she said she wanted an 'understanding about a certain amount of coldness he appeared to have toward her.' She said that everybody was against her including her family at home. Amott told her she was very silly and asked her to get into the trap. She threw a parasol and handbag into the trap and climbed in. She didn't speak, but according to Amott, gazed about her in a curious manner. It started to rain. When they arrived at Cornelian Bay Railway crossing Amott called to a small child to open the gate and they passed through a few minutes after three. According to Amott, Louisa then stood up

---

5   A largely uninhabited hilly area of bushland just north-east of Hobart

in the trap and said she would drown herself. She threw the parasol away and attempted to get out of the vehicle. Amott prevented her from getting out and she sat down and then fell to her knees on the floor of the trap, unconsciousness. Amott stopped the trap and lifted her out onto the grass and called to a passing woman to assist him. She had some brandy and they tried moistening her lips and other attempts at resuscitation were made before Amott drove into Hobart, to the hospital, to get medical aid. Dr Payne refused to attend and said Dr Scott could not go either. Amott found Dr Crouch who refused on the grounds that he had a Board meeting. Finally he found Dr Hardy who agreed to return with him to the place where Louisa lay and he pronounced her dead. He said the police should be called and that was done at once.

Amott said he had known Louisa for four or five years since she had become acquainted with his family. Louisa's parasol was found at the scene, broken. Amott said he didn't know how it came to be broken and that he had not changed his manner towards the girl. The foreman of the duty asked several pertinent questions:

> *"Did you have any struggle or quarrel with the girl?"*
>
> "No"
>
> *"What position did you have towards the girl, a friend, a lover or what?"*
>
> "A friend, sir"
>
> *"She knew you were married?"*
>
> "Oh yes, she visited our house last Sunday. She went out with my daughter, a girl about the same age."
>
> *"Did she take any poison in the trap?"*
>
> "No, I would have noticed it"
>
> *"Did she ever complain of being ill?"*
>
> "Never"

Ann Brown who lived at the Cornelian Bay crossing and was called to help by Amott, gave evidence and said that Amott had told her that Louisa had been in a temper and was threatening to drown herself. She did not see any bottles of a suspicious nature or any signs of a struggle.

Another witness Alexander Saunders said he was driving out to the Cornelian Bay Cemetary on Monday afternoon at about 3.15pm and he saw a trap standing near the football ground. Amott was in the vehicle with a young lady whose head was resting on Amott's knee. She was either in a sitting or kneeling position, he did not see her face and could not say whether she was dead or not. He didn't stop, as he was not asked to do so. He was driving in the same direction as Amott who was in sight for 10 minutes.

The inquest was adjourned until Friday because Dr Hardy's evidence was not complete.

Friday 10th October 1890

The inquest was resumed and doctors Hardy and Payne, who examined Louisa, said that finding her body healthy they thought that death had resulted from sudden excitement or shock. Mr Riddoch, the coroner, said he considered that the doctor's statement regarding the cause to death was unsatisfactory.

The court heard evidence from Dr Hardy. He stated that on Monday 6th October at about 3.35pm he was called by Mr Amott to view the body of Louisa. He found her lying by the side of the road, near the football ground on Risdon Road. He found that she was dead with no marks of violence on her body except for bruising of the right wrist and no smell detected from her mouth. The following day he conducted a post mortem examination and found all the organs healthy except for a small patch of old pericarditis on the outside of the heart. Her stomach contents were examined and no trace of poison found. The coroner questioned the doctor and asked him if he was under the impression from his first examination that Louisa died from some other cause than natural causes and that she had probably administered poison? He replied that from the healthy state of the body he thought she might have taken something.

The foreman of the jury asked if there might have been chloroform on Louisa's handkerchief. The doctor replied that there might have been but there was no odour coming from the deceased's mouth.

Dr Payne then gave his evidence about the post mortem that he carried out with Dr Hardy. He said that the body of the deceased gave all the appearance of being healthy and well nourished. All the organs were healthy, except for the small patch on the heart. The heart had been examined under a microscope and there was no evidence of degeneration of the muscle fibre. He added that the uterus and ovaries were healthy and that the uterus was virgin. The doctor was questioned as to the cause of death and he answered that he had come to no conclusion as to how she had died and any theories would be speculation given that no evidence was found at the post mortem.

There was some question as to the speed or lack of, in the doctor's response to the incident. Apparently Dr Payne and a Dr Scott were working at the hospital and refused to leave and attend the scene when told about Louisa. The foreman of the jury asked Dr Payne if thought that if he had gone to the girl when he was first sent for would she have had a better chance? Dr Payne said this question required a long answer! He said that it was not his duty to leave the hospital and it was not in his or Dr Scott's power to go. They were not allowed to attend 'outside cases'. He added that he was under the impression that Louisa was already dead by the time Mr Amott drove into town with her.

Louisa's father again gave evidence to the court. He said that he was a widower and that Louisa kept house for him together with her sister and grandmother. He was asked if she was unhappy at home and he said that certain anonymous letters that she had recently received had annoyed her. He was asked if he thought they contributed to her state of unhappiness. William said he hadn't realised how great their influence had been until her death. He added that Louisa had told her sister that she would have to leave Tasmania if the letters continued and that she had become a changed person since they started to arrive in June 1889. William said that everything in the letters was untrue and when he had shown her the first letter she was dumbstruck. No mention was made of the content of the letters. He then added that certain rumours have been coupled with Mr Amott but they were all false. He said that Amott had treated his daughter the same as his own. He said he proved that beyond doubt. William added that he was 'funning' with her when he last saw her alive and that they were to have gone away the next day for a short holiday.

The coroner summed up the case. He concluded that the case seemed to be somewhat unsatisfactory given the lack of evidence. He believed that the anonymous letters would have put her into a state of considerable excitement. Mr Amott had also described the state she was in when he met with her and this also may have contributed to her death. The theory about self-poisoning was not proved and he recommended that the jury bring in an open verdict. He even gave them the wording "The said Louisa Brundle did, on October 6th 1890, whilst driving along Bell Street, New Town, suddenly expire but there is no evidence to show how or what means the deceased came by her death". The foreman of the jury said they would consider it. After about 10 minutes the foreman announced that the jury had reached its decision, and they agreed with the Coroner on the verdict he suggested.

There was a lot of information given at the inquest but probably more questions than answers:

How did Louisa get the bruising to her right wrist?

What was in the anonymous letters?

Why did she arrange to meet a married man, twice her age, in the middle of nowhere?

The doctors offered a lot of detail about the state of her organs, including that her uterus was virgin. Presumably this meant she had never borne a child, but they didn't offer any information about whether or not she was sexually active. When I first read about this incident I had suspicions that fell broadly on Thomas Amott. He left town to meet a perfectly healthy young girl in quiet spot and she just died? I had some reservations about the truth of the story, given the evidence.

However, after some research, I have unearthed something that might be a possible explanation.

Sudden Arrhythmic Death Syndrome (SADS) causes a dramatic and sudden cardiac death. It increases instability in the heart's electrical system, which can force the muscle into overdrive ultimately leading to death. This condition often occurs in young people who have no outward signs of ill health and there are two additional factors that make this pertinent to Louisa Brundle's death. 1) SADS is different to sudden cardiac death in that no definite cause of death can be found, even after an expert cardiac pathologist has examined the heart and 2) the weakness is often inherited. Given that Louisa's mother died of 'fright' at the same age this begins to look a likely theory. The condition can be triggered by strenuous exercise or any kind of adrenaline surge, so the fright that Elizabeth suffered and Louisa being upset with Amott could have triggered both these attacks. SADS also appears to be attributed to some cases of 'cot death'. I have no evidence of the cause of death of Charles Henry Brundle, Louisa's brother who died at the age of nine months, but maybe there is also a link there.

Of course it's possible that there are other explanations; the two deaths could be coincidence or other medical conditions might be responsible. However any other condition would need to fulfil the following criteria:
- It affects young adults who show no sign of previous illness.
- It is hereditary
- There is no trace of damage to vital organs at post-mortem

There are still many questions and various scenarios that could have been played out that day ranging from the middle aged philanderer telling his young lover that they should end their affair to the inexperienced young woman with a crush on her friend's father.

Thomas Amott led an interesting life. His obituary in the Hobart Mercury on 4th March 1929 runs to over two pages detailing his achievements. Aged 42 at the time of Louisa's death, he was married to his second wife Annie, and they had 5 children under the age of 6. Altogether he had thirteen children, three from his first marriage and ten from the second. He was ambitious and aggressive in his ambitions, not afraid to take on the establishment, including the local press.

The week following the report of Louisa's inquest this advert appeared in the Mercury:

> *Mr Thomas Amott, Hobart*
>
> *Sir, I beg to express with reference to the death of the late Miss Louisa Brundle, detrimental reports reflecting upon you, were inadvertently allowed to appear in the Launceston Examiner of the 7th and 8th instance, and which reports were not true, as proved by the evidence given in the subsequent inquest on the case referred to. I shall be glad to publish this apology, if you desire it, in the Hobart, Launceston and Melbourne papers, where the above mentioned detrimental reports were circulated. Yours obediently*
>
> *Henry Button,*
>
> *Proprietor of the Launceston Examiner*

The only reports I can find that were published on 7th and 8th October were reports of the inquest at which the foreman of the jury did ask some pointed questions of Amott regarding his relationship with Louisa

The manner of the apology, by Henry Button suggests that Amott was an important man within the community and nobody wanted to upset him. In 1911, Thomas Amott was appointed Mayor of Hobart.

Chasing Rainbows

That brings us almost to the end of the end of Jabez' line in Tasmania. There is a small chance of Tasmanian descendants but only if Eliza Ann Brundle went on to have children and that's a whole other line of research.

Chasing Rainbows

THE ACTOR'S LINE

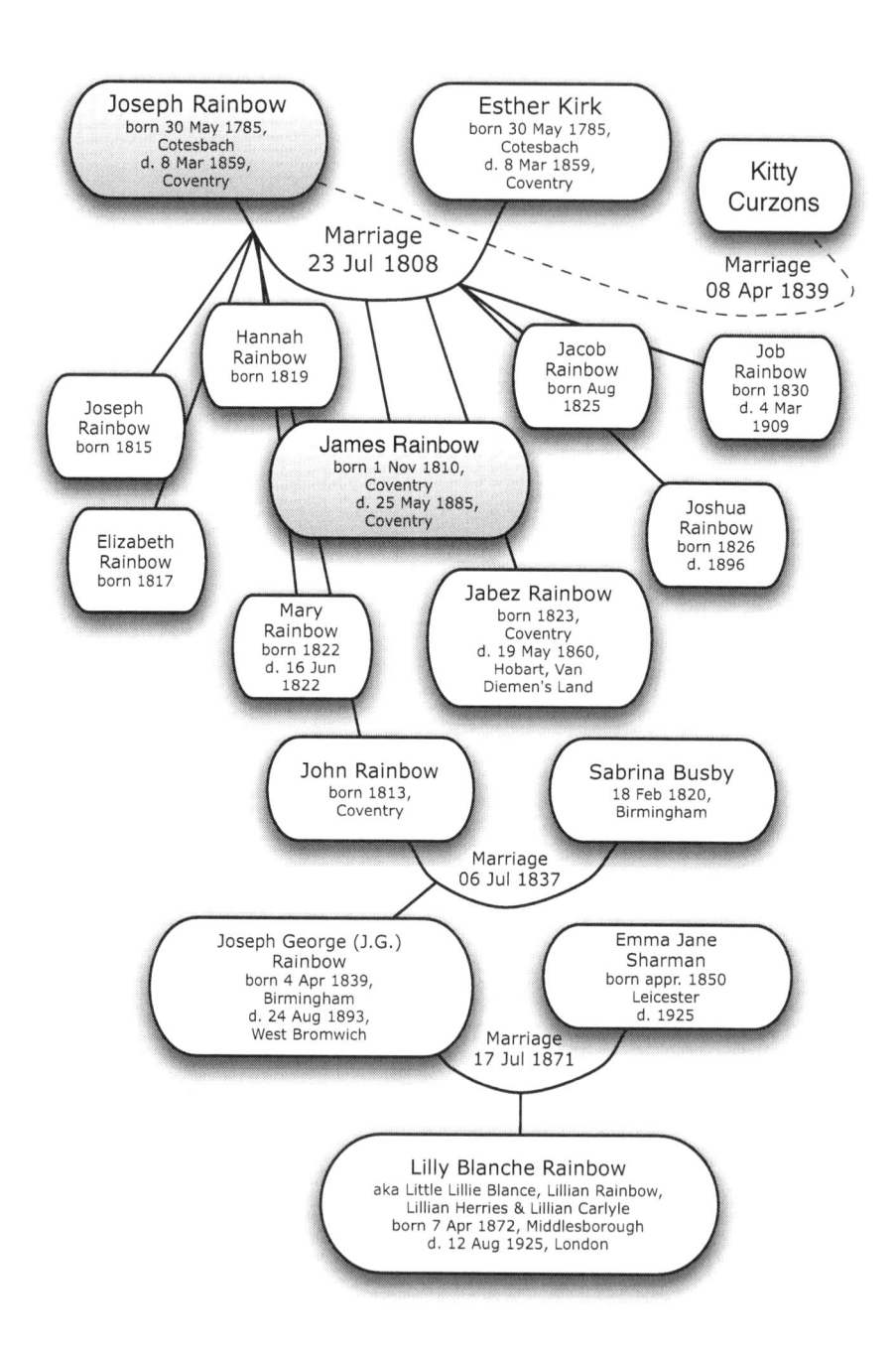

- **Joseph Rainbow** — born 30 May 1785, Cotesbach; d. 8 Mar 1859, Coventry
- **Esther Kirk** — born 30 May 1785, Cotesbach; d. 8 Mar 1859, Coventry
- **Kitty Curzons**

Marriage 23 Jul 1808 (Joseph Rainbow & Esther Kirk)
Marriage 08 Apr 1839 (Joseph Rainbow & Kitty Curzons)

Children of Joseph Rainbow and Esther Kirk:
- **Joseph Rainbow** — born 1815
- **Elizabeth Rainbow** — born 1817
- **Hannah Rainbow** — born 1819
- **James Rainbow** — born 1 Nov 1810, Coventry; d. 25 May 1885, Coventry
- **Mary Rainbow** — born 1822, d. 16 Jun 1822
- **Jabez Rainbow** — born 1823, Coventry; d. 19 May 1860, Hobart, Van Diemen's Land
- **Jacob Rainbow** — born Aug 1825
- **Joshua Rainbow** — born 1826, d. 1896
- **Job Rainbow** — born 1830, d. 4 Mar 1909

- **John Rainbow** — born 1813, Coventry
- **Sabrina Busby** — 18 Feb 1820, Birmingham

Marriage 06 Jul 1837

- **Joseph George (J.G.) Rainbow** — born 4 Apr 1839, Birmingham; d. 24 Aug 1893, West Bromwich
- **Emma Jane Sharman** — born appr. 1850, Leicester; d. 1925

Marriage 17 Jul 1871

- **Lilly Blanche Rainbow** — aka Little Lillie Blance, Lillian Rainbow, Lillian Herries & Lillian Carlyle; born 7 Apr 1872, Middlesborough; d. 12 Aug 1925, London

104

An Actor's Life For Me

Every family historian needs a thespian branch just in case the task of digging through the archives for 'normal' ancestors isn't quite challenging enough! Actors bring with them the added complications of stage names that are used seemingly randomly and the occupational hazard of constantly moving from location to location. To a family historian this often means census information, which can be a vital tool for linking a family together, is either missing or limited. If our actor ancestor is included in a census return at all it's often as a lodger or boarder, giving us no clue as to where he or she fits in with the rest of his or her family.

I've been fortunate with the Rainbow actors in that they have been relatively well documented and as more Victorian publications have been digitised and made available online many of the puzzles from my earlier research have been solved.

As far as I am able to determine, Joseph George, (grandson of Joseph of Cotesbach/Coventry and nephew of Jabez) was the first Rainbow to tread the boards. He was born on 4th April 1839 in Essex Street in the heart of Birmingham. His father, John was a printer's compositor and his mother, Sabrina (nee Busby) was a dressmaker. At the age of 11, Joseph was listed as a pocket book maker in the 1851 census and 10 years later as a printer's compositor, like his father and still living at home.

According to his obituary, he learnt his acting trade at a Birmingham amateur theatrical club. In the census of 1871 and now 32 years old Joseph is recorded at 38 Grafton Street, Leeds, a boarder at a lodging house and listed as a dramatic artist. We only have to look at the events of ten years of our own lives to realise the major changes that can take place during a similar time period and can only speculate as to what drew Joseph away from, what one must imagine was a relatively stable occupation to the vagaries and economic uncertainties of the acting profession. A few months after the census on July 17th 1871 Joe married Emma. Emma Jane Sharman was born in Leicester around 1850, the daughter of Joseph and Grace. In the 1871 census she was listed as a machinist living with her parents at 11, Southampton Street, Leicester.

In the 19th century the occupation of a provincial actor was far from the glamourous lifestyle we associate with show business these days. For the fortunate few it was possible to make a dramatic 'rags to riches' transition in the profession, but most actors were underemployed and poorly paid, sustaining themselves on little above starvation wages. Even on this lowly remuneration, subsidy of theatre management was usually a requirement and it has been suggested that an actor who could provide not only his own costumes but a generous selection of props, make up and accessories was half way to securing an engagement. This was even more of a burden for women, as dresses were never provided and were a major expense.

No expenses were paid to the actors for accommodation and they were often expected to supply their own publicity, for example, by fly-posting the town. Play scripts were often limited and were shared amongst the cast with members copying out additional scripts in the time available outside rehearsals. The burgeoning rail network of the 1850s allowed for ease of travelling between provincial theatres and greater employment opportunities outside London but again rail travel was not cheap and actors of the travelling 'stock' companies often had to dip into savings or acquire loans to survive.

The purchase of a trade paper was also a prerequisite for any actor who was serious about acquiring employment. The Era was a weekly newspaper, published between 1837 and 1939 that evolved into the principal theatre publication of its time; its modern equivalent would be 'The Stage'. The Rainbow family appear often in the newspaper from the late 1860's to the 1900's, either advertising their productions, looking for employment, or in reviews of their shows. It was in an advertisement on the front page of The Era, on March 2nd 1873 that

I found the first mention of J.G. (as he was to be known - Joe to his friends) and Emma together:

Entire Lead or Secondary Business and Walking Ladies

Mr J G Rainbow and Miss Emma Rainbow at Liberty to arrange for the above

Address: Sadler's Wells Theatre, Islington, N.

Sadler's Wells is a name that conjures up visions of grandeur and the upper echelons of theatrical society. How exciting then to think that Joe and Emma must have been doing so well at that time. However, a quick look at the history of the Sadler's Wells theatre reveals a slightly different story (and a swift reminder not to make assumptions!) From its former glory days in the middle of the 19th century when its Shakespeare productions were much acclaimed it had fallen into decline and the very year after Joe and Emma gave the theatre as their address there were plans to turn the site into a bathhouse. Maybe it was not quite such a prestigious beginning to their careers.

During the 1870's they toured the country - London, Dover and Carlisle in 1873; Preston, Doncaster and Bolton in 1874. After Bolton, on 5th June 1874 they placed an advertisement in The Era looking for work saying that they had been 'disengaged through a misunderstanding' and giving their address as 11 Southampton Street, Leicester (the home of Emma's parents). I can't find any clue as to what this misunderstanding may have been, although after this incident Emma was referred to as *Miss Emma Rainbow* with the addition of *(Mrs R)* after her name in their advertisements in The Era. Was this a coincidence or was J.G. making it very clear that Emma was his wife because of the 'misunderstanding'?

By August of that year they were back in London and in employment, working at the East London Theatre and then onto the Marylebone Theatre for a 21-month engagement. One of the Marylebone plays was The Outcasts of London where Joe played a character called Herr Vonn Volterchoker and a reviewer commented "...although Mr Rainbow makes no attempt at a German accent he succeeded in winning frequent laughter by the use of the vernacular."

July 1876 and they were advertising for work again, citing their time at the Marylebone and including extracts from favourable press critiques. In August they returned to the Marylebone and remained until the following summer, when they moved to the Theatre Royal Grimsby for a 42 week season, followed by a season at the Theatre Royal in Birmingham in the autumn of 1879.

The plays in which Emma and Joe performed were mostly Victorian melodramas which were filled with every element designed to appeal to the theatre going public; suspense, mystery, high emotion, implausible story lines, life lessons, tragedy and romance.

Provincial theatre-going in the late 19th century was not the exclusive domain of the middle classes as it became in later years and the melodrama could be compared to the modern day TV soap opera. Favourite productions became established, such as East Lynne, which was hugely popular both in Britain and the USA. This elaborate story of mistaken identity became so successful that it was an almost guaranteed moneymaker with theatre managers who used it to pull in a crowd at the end of less successful run. It was also a popular choice of play for an actor's 'benefit'. 'Benefit' performances were an important part of an actor's income; a chance to supplement their pay by taking home between a third to a half of a night's takings. Although the practice had died out in London during the 1860's, it was still going strong in Emma & Joe's time in the provinces and several reviews in The Era make mention of a play being performed for Miss Rainbow's benefit.

To use the benefit system to it's best advantage an actor had to make him or herself popular with the public throughout the engagement and curry favour with everyone in the locality to encourage the best possible turn out for his or her performance. There were also expenses involved for the actor - the theatre manager would level set charges to accommodate the benefit plus assorted charges for props, extras and possibly even hospitality towards prospective patrons.

On 20th October 1879 J.G. Rainbow, Miss Emma Rainbow and Miss Lillie Blanche are made first appearance together at the Star Theatre, Bury. Lillie Blanch was Joe and Emma's only child - but more about the elusive Miss Lillie and her movable date of birth later.

Child actors were common in the Victorian theatre. Acting was largely a family affair due to the nature of the travelling stock company and it was rare for actors to marry 'outsiders'. The unusual hours and travel would put a strain on any marriage but sustaining a relationship with someone outside the world of the theatre would prove almost impossible. Theatrical dynasties were formed with the husband and wife as lead actors and extended family members making up the bulk of the rest of the company with children acting as soon as they were old enough.

Marriages between theatrical families were common and as actors were often treated with suspicion by wider society these tight-knit and isolated family units gave the acting community stability and support. They looked after their own. The children invariably drifted into the same occupation as their parents and hopefully, being family members, they were treated better than the children written about in an article from The Era, 1885.

Children aged 4 to 12 are described as being taken to theatres by their parents to act in the Christmas pantomimes and are 'roughly drilled by the super-master and ballet-masters'. 'They are pushed here and thrust there like nine pins.' The writer justifies this because the 'material was rarely good' and that anyway the children were accustomed to receiving harsher treatment in their everyday lives. The children's dressing area was an unheated space under the stage and their costumes stored on damp walls. The long and tedious rehearsals and incessant bawling of the stage manager was part of the discipline, which was seen as "no hardship".

The article goes on to berate the School Board officials who visited the theatre looking for young truants for pressurising the children. Neither parents nor theatre management had any love for the Board and the writer describes the 'sweet employment of dodging the School Board's functionaries'. He finishes by suggesting that after the first few nights the small actors would enjoy themselves on stage as much as the children in the audience.

The sentiments expressed may appear shocking to our twenty-first century sensibilities, but given the context, Dickensian London and the prevalent attitudes towards childhood, he may have been correct that the children were more kindly treated at the theatre than at home or on the street.

By 1881 the census tells us that Joe and Emma were living at 13 Cleveland Street, Wolverhampton. Joe is listed as aged 41 and a theatrical actor as is his wife, Emma Jane, aged 31. Lillie Blanche was 8...maybe.

According to his obituary it was around this time that Joe progressed into theatre management, taking on theatres in Shrewsbury and Bridlington Quay with some success. The family also toured with several plays: *Proved True* by Mortimer Murdoch and two plays *The Main Hope* and *Lucky Star*, specially written for them by a member of the Shrewsbury theatre, George Comer,. In a theatrical gossip column of the September 26th 1885 the Era writes that 'Miss Emma Rainbow, manageress of *Proved True* company purchased the sole London and provincial rights of *The Main Hope* from author, Mr George Comer.'

These three melodramas feature heavily in the Era both as advertisements and reviews. In 1883 the Era wrote of the company appearing at the Lyceum Theatre, Crewe "Mr Levey is evidently doing his best to keep faith with the public of Crewe in his promise to bring first-class talent to the above, and we have this week had a splendid treat by the introduction of Mr and Mrs Rainbow, who opened on Monday evening with *Proved True*, in which Mrs Rainbow as Liz Tabner and Mr Rainbow as Robert Thynne were remarkably successful and fully deserved the continued applause accorded them....Miss Lillie Blanche as Archie and La Petite Moya Kean as Little Harry were very good and taken as a whole, it is one of the best companies we have ever had in Crewe. *Bess* and *East Lynne* (uh oh!) are announced for the latter part of the week.

On November 3rd 1883, Joe took over as lessee and manager of the Theatre Royal, West Bromwich. Fred Bennett, in his history of the theatre devotes a chapter to Rainbow's stewardship. Joe was no stranger to either the theatre or the area and the book informs us that he is 'an actor of considerable experience' and 'father of Miss Emma Rainbow, whose company had been regular visitors to the Theatre Royal.' This statement puzzled me initially, particularly as the father/daughter relationship is repeated throughout the chapter. I have concluded that this was either originally a typo or misunderstanding that has been picked up and replicated. Although Joe did act with his child, it was Lillie Blanche and not Emma who was his daughter. According to every official document, census, marriage certificate and newspaper advertisement Emma was most definitely his wife. One possibility may be, that as she was ten years younger and shared the same surname, it was assumed by the local journalist that she must be his daughter. Apart from that inaccuracy, Bennett thoroughly documents the nine years that the family managed the Royal, based on research from local newspapers of the era.

During the summer before the Rainbows arrived, considerable alterations had taken place to the theatre including new dressing rooms, an extension to the stage, reseating and the interior being completely redecorated. Joe appears to have started with a clean sweep, receiving letters of praise over his insistence on maintaining good order in what could be a rowdy and drunken environment and his ban on smoking. New lines were introduced into the concert hall scenes: 'Why is this theatre like the sky after a shower of rain when the sun is shining?" the reply came, "because there's a Rainbow in it" and the response 'May that Rainbow shine in West Bromwich for many years to come". According to The Weekly News the audience greeted this line with enthusiastic applause.

Chasing Rainbows

November 1883 would prove to be an unforgettable month for Emma and Joe. As her husband was taking over as manager of the Royal, Emma was on tour with her own company and two weeks later, on the last night of a run in Darlington the theatre manager arranged for fireworks to be set off to mark the occasion. Unfortunately the theatre caught fire and burnt down, causing over £6,000's worth of damage. Although the building was insured this did not include the props and costumes belonging to Emma's company and the local newspaper reported the following week that local people had held a collection for Miss Rainbow in order to help with the replacement of all her pantomime costumes.

This was not to be the only experience of fire for the Rainbows. During their first pantomime season at the Royal, one evening after the performance had ended, a fire broke out on stage. The actors quickly put the blaze out but the fire brigade was called as a precautionary measure and a man was left in the theatre overnight in case it reignited. There were no further outbreaks and the damage was estimated at £200. The Rainbows were not unusually unlucky or careless - theatre fires were common in the Victorian era. The new gas lighting created a serious hazard and in the last 30 years of the 19th century there were 91 major fires reported in theatres with many performers being killed or injured.

In January 1884, two months after the Rainbows took over in West Bromwich Emma made her first appearance under the new management playing the part of *Leah*, another Victorian favourite and a role made famous by the American born actress Kate Bateman. The local paper was enthusiastic:

> *"Comparisons are objectionable, but Miss Rainbow is certainly as acceptable as the acknowledged great representative of the part, Miss Bateman."*

A month later *She Stoops To Conquer* was performed for Emma's benefit. After the show ended the auditorium was cleared and a transformation took place; carpets were laid down to the Queen Street entrance and the theatre was elaborately decorated for a farewell dance held to mark Miss Rainbow's impending provincial tour with her own company.

While his wife was touring provincial towns with her own productions Joe also turned his hand to writing, in addition to his acting and theatre management duties. In November of 1885 a new drama, *In The Dead of Night*, was performed at the Royal. It was partly based on a novel serialised in the West Bromwich Weekly News, '*The Shadows on the Blind*' written by Edward C. Matthews, an actor in the company and J.C. Rainbow.

Sensation, sentiment and spectacle were surely the keywords of the provincial Victorian theatre and if the show didn't have a theme of orphans to draw a tear, it would be a dramatic fight sequence or some extraordinary mechanical effect to captivate the audience. *Proved True*, for example, featured an astonishing rescue scene from a sinking ship complete with thrashing sails and water. The plays were not without unintentional humour. In *The Era* (of Saturday, July 5, 1884) the reviewer gleefully recounts that 'in the last act of *Proved True* there is a double scene, embracing interior and exterior. The villain of the play was seen eavesdropping and the audience was breathless, when a voice from the front cried, "He's listening outside!" There was a roar of laughter not intended by the author.'

In 1887 Emma's company performed another play especially written for her by George Comer, *The Lucky Star*. The publicity surrounding the show wouldn't seem out of place today, with men being seen around town with a silver star attached to their watch chain, ladies wearing star brooches and children with paper windmills in the shape of a star all bearing the logo '*Lucky Star*' until the town was buzzing with the question, "What does Lucky Star mean?".

In West Bromwich, in addition to the traditional plays, Joe was staging a variety of events to pull in the crowds from football contests involving the local West Bromwich Albion squad to the Midget Minstrels a troupe of 24 little boys and girls, the boys performing with blacked faces.

In October 1891 Emma performed *'The Main Hope'* at West Bromwich. There had been major renovations since the fire and with the enlargement of the stage the ship scene and lighthouse were reproduced on a more elaborate scale than ever attempted before. The breaking up of the vessel occupied the entire set. The local newspaper reported that the play had been modified and improved several times since it was introduced at West Bromwich theatre, but an important alteration had been made this time in the plot. Instead of being killed when the ship was blown up, the villain escaped and died, repentant, in the last act. "This alteration was suggested by Mr. Rainbow on the grounds that the piece was practically at an end in the death of the villain and we confess that it has made a wonderful improvement."

The successful partnership between Joe and Emma ended on 24th August 1893. Joe had suffered from pneumonia, but after returning from a holiday in Jersey he seemed to have recovered to a great extent. However that evening, he was standing at the front door of the theatre chatting 'in his well known genial manner to some friends' when he was seized with pains. He was helped to bed but after rising a short time later he collapsed again and died. He was 54. The theatre was closed and Emma and Lillie, who were playing at Wolverhampton, were sent for. The funeral took place on Monday 28th August. Joe's coffin was transported on a carriage pulled by his own pony and was so laden with wreaths and flowers that the coffin was completely hidden from view. The Weekly News published a poem and a comment:

"Under Mr. Rainbow's management the local theatre has been greatly improved. It has been his aim all along, in which he has met with a large amount of success and has gained the support of many of those who have been accustomed to give their patronage to the Birmingham theatres."

The Stage of 31st August reported his death and added:

"Great sympathy is felt for Mrs Rainbow and her daughter Miss Lillie Rainbow, to whom the shock was most terrible. The latter were playing at The Star, Wolverhampton, when the news was communicated to them and they did not reach home until midnight."

The Era published an obituary written by a friend,

"As a tribute of respect, one may be permitted to say a word as to the actor-manager whose sudden death caused such a shock to his friends, and they were legion. It is not given to many men, either in or out of the profession to be so popular and to be so genuinely liked as was the late Mr J.G. Rainbow, or as his intimates called him, and as he liked to be called, "Joe Rainbow". Being one of the old school of actors whom few - very few - are now left, and being both a resident and travelling manager, his name was a household word in the profession; but amongst the vast number of his friends and acquaintances there would not be found one who could justly say a word against him. He was so innately kind-hearted and had such a fund of good humour that everyone of necessity, liked him, and everyone who had business relations with him found that his word was as good as his bond...

He was continually urged to be a Town Councillor, but his heart and soul were in his profession, and to that only he cared to confine his attention. Many a one will miss his kindly greeting at the theatre. His quips and cranks and amusing anecdotes made him 'good company'. Dullness would not reign where he was: and even throughout this year, when he was tortured by a wretched cough, he ever sustained his genial good spirits. King Death is rapidly thinning the ranks of the old school of actors; the loss of any one of them is a matter for regret; for it weakens a profession that is now jumped into rather than learnt....

There are two persons in particular to whom this loss will be irreparable: may those two persons understand that they have the condolences and heartfelt sympathy of all who were considered friends of poor Joe Rainbow. Your obedient servant, REMOC. September 11th 1893." [6]

In September Emma announced that she would not continue to manage the theatre and Mr James Page Moore would be taking over.

After Joe's death Emma continued to tour, both with her own company and others including Osmond Tearle's Shakespearean

---

6 see appendix

company. She was an admired and respected actor according to the press reviews as witnessed by this small compilation published in The Stage in March 1881.

In Wolverhampton, Opinions of the Local Press

Upon Miss Emma Rainbow devolved the impersonation of the bright and mirthful, although pardonably deceitful Miss Hardcastle, and the lady throughout the piece showed that she had carefully studied her part, and that it was one for which she was eminently fitted - Express October 30, 1880.

The Lady of Lyons, in which the charming and artistic acting of Miss Emma Rainbow, was the strongest point. Express Nov 12 1880

We have much pleasure in presenting our readers with a portrait of Miss Emma Rainbow, a lady well known in the theatrical world, and who is at present engaged at the Prince of Wales's Theatre. We have had the pleasure of witnessing several of Miss Rainbow's pleasing impersonations, and it is only justice to say that in every part undertaken she seems perfectly at home, showing evidence of a perfect grasp of the author's meaning, and her clear ringing voice, faultless enunciation, graceful figure and prepossessing appearance add greatly to the pleasure of witnessing even the highest class productions. Last night in Bulwer Lyttons celebrated play of the Lady of Lyons, Miss Rainbow took the difficult part of "Pauline" in a manner that greatly added to her high reputation, and would have satisfied a much more critical audience then we can ever hope to see brought together at any Wolverhampton Theatre. Magpie Nov 13th 1880.

Of course the reviews were not all good, the following paragraph from an 1889 edition of the Manchester Times was particularly scathing about the specially written 'Lucky Star':

> "St. James's Theatre - A company under the direction of Miss Emma Rainbow commenced a week's engagement at St. James's Theatre on Monday evening 'Lucky Star' the drama which they produced is not a play of much merit. It consists of several scenes of ordinary melodramatic character but is relieved from utter mediocrity by some spirited situations supposed to be enacted in the Soundan" (sic).

However, Emma continued to tour with this play until 1899 when she had the last laugh, as this report in The Era of 1899 reports:

> "Mr D'Oyly Carte has been 'twitted' in several quarters because he did not sooner announce the title of the new Savoy opera. The fact of the matter is, the name fixed upon was already known in the provinces as that of a highly sensational melodrama. Only two days before the production of The Lucky Star at the Savoy was Mr D'Oyly Carte able to complete negotiations for the purchase of the right to use the title, including the play itself, from Miss Emma Rainbow, the lucky possessor of both."

I can't help but wonder if the last minute nature of these negotiations was because Emma was holding out for a great price. Unfortunately I've been unable to find a record of the transaction itself. The new operetta produced under the name *Lucky Star* was not particularly successful and ended after a short run at The Savoy.

The use of the word 'twitted' is interesting given the recent popularity of the social networking service, Twitter. However the old fashioned definition is a derivative of the word 'twit' meaning fool or idiot and twitted, in this context, means "...to taunt, ridicule, or tease, especially for embarrassing mistakes or faults."

We can see an example of an attempt to make a twit out of Mr D'Oyly Carte in an article written by a rather indignant journalist in The Stage, 12th January 1899:

Chasing Rainbows

> "I never could understand why some managers will persist in keeping back the name of a new piece until the eleventh hour. It is always a dangerous proceeding for full publicity is wise in such cases in order that there may be no infringement of title. Look at the case of The Lucky Star, produced at the Savoy on Saturday night. It was only on the day before it saw the light that Mr D'Olyly Carte vouchsafed to give the title to the public, and the result is that he has hit upon a name which is familiar throughout the provinces in connection with the play that Miss Emma Rainbow has been touring with for goodness knows how many years. If Mr Carte had consulted the columns of The Stage he would have steered clear of the regrettable blunder. As it is, I suppose he must alter the name of his play unless Miss Rainbow is generous and willing enough to give up the title."

This is swiftly followed in the following week's Stage by:

> "With reference to a paragraph of mine in last week's issue Mr. D'Oyly Carte has written to me.. 'we were well aware another piece existed under the title The Lucky Star and we have been for some time in negotiation to purchase the piece and its title, which negotiations were only completed two days before the production of The Lucky Star at the Savoy Theatre.' This may be so, but it does not do away with the fact that managers, as a rule, are most loth to announce the title of a new piece in decent time before production; neither does it prove than in future whenever The Lucky Star is presented local playgoers will take it to be the melodrama toured for many years by Miss Emma Rainbow.
>
> Miss Emma Rainbow has also written to me on the same subject. In the course of her letter she says: - I should be very glad if you would kindly make known through your columns that I have sold the drama The Lucky Star

> *to Mr D'Oyly Carte, and that both piece and title are now, of course, his property. My play had a very long and successful run. It was truly "lucky" to me and I sincerely wish Mr D'Oyly Carte every possible success with his Lucky Star."*

It would seem that badly researched journalism is not a modern phenomenon after all.

Searching through the archives of *The Stage* for Emma Rainbow produces over 800 hits. These are, for the most part, either advertisements for plays she is producing, looking for theatres to host her productions, or reviews of her work. She acted and produced consistently all over the British Isles from her early twenties through to her sixties. The last mention of her career appears to be this entry in the May 29th 1919 edition of The Stage:

> *Miss Emma Rainbow, Disengaged, 21 Fawcett Street, Redcliffe Gardens, London, SW10.*

The last play, at least one that was advertised in The Stage appears to be this one published on May 31st 1917:

> *Miss Emma Rainbow. Re-engaged by Mr Charles Draycott for Mrs Austin in "His Love For An Actress".*

Emma died in Romford, Essex in 1925 at the age of 76 just weeks after her daughter. Sadly I cannot find any obituary for her in either *The Era* or *The Stage* and I don't know if she had any extended family or, in fact, what her circumstances were at the end of her life. We can only hope that she lived out the last years in comfort, maybe buffered by the proceeds of her Lucky Star.

Lilly Blanche RAINBOW

Genfile

Profile

In brief

Lilly Blanche Rainbow, known professionally as Lillian Herries was a Victorian actress, touring both in Britain and abroad.

Known for...

having difficulties with remembering her own age. She appears on various documents with many different dates of birth.

Events

Year	
1879	'Little Lillie Blanche' took to the stage with her parents, J.G. and Emma Rainbow, for the first time aged about seven.
1899	Lillian toured South Africa with the Shakespearean theatre company of Osmond Tearle with favourable reviews.
1916	Lillian married Vincent W. Carlyle. He was an actor/producer/manager and a fellow member of the Actor's Association.

The enigma that is Lillie Blanche Rainbow

Lillie Blanche/Lily Blanche/Lillian Rainbow/Herries/Carlyle was the only daughter of Joseph (J.G.) Rainbow and Emma Rainbow. She has been a difficult woman to pin down even if we start at the beginning with what should be relatively simple, her year of birth. She is the perfect example of why we can't totally rely on official documentation to establish basic facts as mistakes are transcribed, re-transcribed and people don't tell the complete truth, for all sorts of reasons. I haven't been able to find any official record of Lily's birth at all, under any combination of her names so establishing when she was born is dependent on other sources.

The official documentation variously records her as being born in 1869, 1873, 1884 and 1888; a substantial discrepancy range of 19 years.

- Her death certificate informs us that she died in 1925 aged 56 = born 1869
- The 1881 census tells us that she was aged 8 = born 1873
- The 1891 census tells us that she was aged 18 = born 1873
- 20 years later and the 1911 census tells us that she was aged 23 (!) = born 1888
- Her marriage certificate states that she was 32 in 1916 = born 1884

We can probably discount both the marriage certificate age and the 1911 census info as this would mean she was born several years *after* the census where she was recorded as aged 8! I'm sure the practice of actresses being economical with the truth when it came to their age must have been as common in Victorian times as it is now. In reality, she might have been a little older than her 41 year old groom and maybe this was an incentive to deduct a decade.

So maybe the death certificate is more reliable? Maybe, but the accuracy of the information on Lillian's death certificate is also questionable. It was supplied by Harry Aynsleigh, a cousin and he informed the registrar that she was a spinster, even though we have a record of her marriage to Vincent Carlyle in 1916.

Both the census entries are consistent and from some additional information I think this is likely to be more accurate. In 'The Stage' on Thursday April 21st 1892 a paragraph reads:

> *"At the conclusion of her engagement last week at the Royal, Middlesbrough, Miss Emma Rainbow presented the proprietors, Messers Geo and C. Imeson, each with a handsome cigar case in commemoration of her daughter's (Miss Lillie Herries) birthday, who was born in Middlesbrough 20 years ago."*

1872 then, would seem likely to the be the most accurate estimate of her date of birth and with a little more detective work I found that in April of that year Mr J. G. Rainbow was acting manager for Mr & Clousten Foster's Comedy and Burlesque Company and Troupe of Champion Knights who were appearing at the Theatre Royal, Middlesborough from April 1st for 12 nights. The troupe moved onto Darlington after this, so assuming that Lillie's mother, Emma was travelling round with Joseph, it looks like Lillie was born sometime during the first 12 days of April. (Update: I discovered today, from the 'Happy Returns of the Day' column in the April 1st 1897 edition of The Stage that Lillie was born on April 7th.)

Lillie's place of birth had also been contentious with some 'place of birth' information being difficult to read on census returns, but this article also seems to confirm that she was born in Middlesborough, albeit if only passing through. The civil registration of births in Middlesborough are complicated by the fact that it did not become it's own registration district until 1875 and before that date, back as far as 1837 when national registration began, it was part of the Stockton registration district. All this seems irrelevant, however because Lillie's birth record is nowhere to be found and it could be that she just didn't get registered at all, which wasn't uncommon at this time.

In 1879 at the tender age of seven, 'Little Lillie Blanche' started performing as a child actress along with her parents, the first occasion being in Bury. Researching Victorian actors is helped enormously by being able to access the digitised archives of two publications devoted to the theatre world, *The Era* and *The Stage* and it was from those records that I was able to see that 'Little Lillie Blanche' worked consistently through her childhood up until about the age of 14 when she changed her stage name from Little Lillie Blanche to Lillie Herries and then, several years later, to Lillian Herries.

It was only by a lucky chance that I found an article linking Miss Lillian Herries to her acting parents, Joseph and Emma Rainbow and I was then able to go back and discover her work during the latter part of the 19th century. As far as I can tell, she took the name Lillian Herries from a character in a popular play; *Heroes* and she used it consistently throughout the rest of her career, although her legal name of Rainbow does resurface on official documents. I have not been able to find any family connection with the name Herries, so it would seem to be simply a stage name.

Although J.G. And Emma had established successful careers it appears that Lillie was striving towards independence by not using the family name and by finding engagements away from her family's touring company. In the November 1899 article in *The Era* about Miss Lillian Herries it reports that:

> "She had some experience as a child actress under her father's management. After his death Mrs Emma Rainbow, sold the lease of the theatre, and continued touring companies... She [Lillian] understudied and played leading parts with her mother's company in *Lucky Star, Wheel of Time* and *Proved True*. But, being anxious for more practice and experience in acting than could be obtained with touring companies, Miss Herries secured engagements to play in various stock seasons... During twelve months 'stock' she played a great variety of parts, ranging from tragedy to comedy and drama to

farce... In September 1898 Miss Herries was engaged by Mr Osmond Tearle to support him in the whole round of Shakespearian repertoire."

OSMOND TEARLE

Lillian worked with Osmond Tearle from 1898 until his death in September 1901.

Tearle was an old school Shakespearean actor, born in Devon and raised in Liverpool. Although he gained little popularity in London he earned a good reputation in the provinces and later in the USA. He was a tall man with a dignified presence and known for his precise elocution. According to the biography of the American theatre manager, Charles Frohman (Charles Frohman: Manager and Man, Isaac Frederick Marcosson and Daniel Frohman, 1916, Harper and Brothers, New York and London), Tearle was 'New York's leading matinee idol'. In 1883 Frohman was looking to produce the play 'The Stranglers of Paris' and said, "We've got to get a good cast. I will not be satisfied with anybody but Tearle". However when he approached Tearle's manager, Lester Wallick with the proposition he was told, "Mr Tearle is the handsomest man in New York, and if I loaned him to you to play the ugliest man ever put on stage he would lose his drawing power for me."

Along with his good looks Tearle also had a reputation as a 'ladies man' as documented by the New York Times when his first wife sued him for divorce. He married Mary Alice Rowe in Liverpool, 1871 and they had five children. Two survived, George Osmond Tearle Jr and Beatrice. According to his own admission Osmond was unfaithful to Mary beginning shortly after their wedding with numerous unnamed women. In 1883, as he sailed to begin a new life in America he wrote an extraordinary letter to Mary telling her that their marriage was over and that he was in love with another woman, and had been for two years. He describes the feeling of "repugnance" he experienced when returning home to Liverpool and his astonishment at how she had calmly borne his indiscretions because "in other matters, you have shown spirit." He describes how he would provide for her and the children, (£25 a month for her and £25 for the children) and warns her against following him to America because "it would be exceedingly foolish" and only make matters worse. He went on to caution her that America "is a very inhospitable country to women and I should necessarily have to be very cruel to you. Besides I am taking out my papers as an American citizen and should then obtain a divorce, a thing easily procured here with money and influence." As if all this wasn't bad enough, he adds insult to injury by saying "I am not, nor ever have been, worthy of you and many a time have said I would give, were I the possessor of it, untold gold, could I only even like you." He ends the letter by saying how he had suffered greatly from writing it - "it has made me ill" and he had not been able to sleep.

Poor Osmond! However, Mary was not to be put off by the dramatics, and four months later she had borrowed $200, made her way to New York and had begun the process of suing Osmond for divorce in the Supreme Court citing his letter as evidence. She told the court that she had been left destitute and that Osmond had only paid her $200 since he had written the letter in January. Mary proceeded to inform the court of her husband's earnings: $200 a week for eight months of the year from Wallick's theatre, a benefit that never brings in less than $1,000 and a supplemental summer season which she estimated to bring his total annual earnings to $11,400. She asked for alimony of $75 a week plus $1,000 for expenses and $200 to cover the cost of travelling to America. Initially she was awarded somewhat less, $2,000 a year plus her legal and travel expenses. However, at a further hearing before a referee Mary Tearle's lawyer strongly denounced Tearle for his behaviour in telling his wife not only that he didn't love her but that he even found it impossible to like her. Added to this was the implication that he had libelled the American people by suggesting that influential men would be treated differently to friendless women. Even though a sworn affidavit was presented on behalf of Tearle claiming that his popularity, and therefore earnings, had diminished since the start of the divorce suit Mary's alimony was increased to $3,000. The moral of the story? If you can't be nice at least don't put it in writing!

There was more controversy to come. In the Oxford Dictionary of National Biography it records that Osmond married Marianne (Minnie) Levy, the *widowed* daughter of New York theatrical manager, F.B. Conway. In fact Marianne was not a widow but had her marriage to the famous cornetist Jules Levy annulled, on the grounds that Levy was a bigamist and had a previous wife, who he had never divorced. Levy claimed that Minnie knew of his situation before they were married and as she had now, publicly, made their children illegitimate he could be shot of the whole batch of them! In the New York Times of 28th July 1883 it was reported that Levy had asked the journalist,

> *"Did you read the article in the New York Times of Thursday about an actor's divorce suit in which the Judge delivered a severe reprimand to the man? That man has been an intimate of my wife. It is my suspicion that she now wants to marry that man - all obstacles being removed."*

Levy was right. Only three days later, on 31st July 1883 at The Windsor Hotel, Denver, Colorado, Osmond Tearle married Minnie Conway. The New York Times reports that it caused a sensation in Denver and "efforts are being made to keep the details of the marriage quiet."

In August 1885 Osmond concluded his American engagements and returned to tour the provincial theatres of Britain, once again. Osmond and Minnie acted together and did the rounds of the provinces for a number of years although Minnie disappears from the advertisements in 1888. She died in 1896 but there is no announcement of her death in the stage papers.

After a short break it appears that Osmond reformed his Shakespeare company which, at various times, included both Lillian Herries and her mother, Emma Rainbow. In 1899 Osmond and Lillian joined the Leonard Rayne and Alfred Paumier company and they sailed to South Africa to perform in Cape Town and Johannesburg. From a report in The Era of March 25th 1899:

Chasing Rainbows

> "The Leonard Rayne and Alfred Paumier company will leave Waterloo Station at 11.40am today enroute for Southampton where they join the SS Moor sailing at 4.00pm for Cape Town. The company includes Misses Maude Digby, Amy Grace, Hulo Hodgson, Lillian Herries, Mabel Ormsby, Marie De Burgh and Messrs Leonard Rayne, Alfred Paumier, Osmond Tearle, Frank Beresford, Fred Lane, Sydney Vereker, Fenton Forde and Charles Combe. The rest of the company sailed by the Mexican a fortnight ago."

They toured to good reviews such as this one in the Johannesburg Sportman and Dramatic News of November 1899:

> "Miss Lillian Herries' interpretation of the Queen is a most happy one. She has the entire sympathy of the audience from her first entrance and her artistic performance of a somewhat trying role stamps her as one of the most finished actresses we have yet seen on the Rand. Her voice is particularly sweet, her elocution perfect, and she herself is altogether charming."

The troupe returned after six months in South Africa on 21st October 1899 and they continued with their tour of the English provinces producing Shakespearean plays such as Hamlet and Othello. Lillian was the leading lady to Osmond's leading man, with Emma taking more minor roles. The archives of provincial nineteenth century newspapers record many reviews of the plays including:

> *The Dundee Courier, January 26th 1899*
>
> "Miss Lillian Herries made a most charming Portia. She is happier in comedy than in tragedy. Nothing daintier and prettier could be imagined than her acting in the scene where Bassanio successfully makes his choice and in the trial scene she rose to the occasion admirably.

> *Miss Herries seemed thoroughly to enjoy the part, and therefore played it with wonderful perfection."*
>
> *The Courier and Argus, Dundee Friday 26th January 1900*
>
> *"Miss Lillian Herries made a sweetly girlish Parthenia. She intensified the innocent fresh side of the character, and made it full of charm. Her singing of the verse which ends with the famous line -*
>
> *'Two souls with but a single thought,*
>
> *Two hearts that beat as one.'*
>
> *was particularly effective, especially when sung off the stage and repeated by Mr Tearle in front of the audience."*

Osmond's troupe toured consistently up until May 23rd 1901 when it was reported that:

> *"Mr Osmond Tearle is taking a well earned holiday. Miss Lillian Herries who has been very successful as Mr Tearle's leading lady will tour with a repertory including Fruo Frou, The Profligate, The Notorious Mrs Ebbsmith and other plays. Mr Herbert J. Montague is acting for Miss Herries in arranging the tour."*

Osmond Tearle died in 1901. He had resumed his theatre productions and his company were playing in Newcastle on Tyne. There is a story that his name is linked with the naming of an English northern town. Apparently Tearle requested to be buried in St. Paul's churchyard, Whitley. However, his coffin was taken down the coast to the town of Whitby, apparently a frequent mistake in Victorian times. A competition was held in the local newspaper and the town renamed to Whitley Bay. I can't give any reliance to the provenance of that story, so it's pure speculation. In his will he left £233.

Osmond's stepson - Minnie Conway and Jules Levy's son - went on to become a star of the silent movies in Hollywood working under the name of Conway Tearle. He successfully made the transition to 'talking pictures' and lived in a mansion nestled beneath the famous Hollywood Hills. The building was preserved and is now owned by the American Society of Cinematographers.

Lillian continued to tour and act with her own company and others until her marriage to Vincent W. Carlyle in 1916. He was an actor/manager/producer and a member of the Actor's Association. Lillian had become an elected member of the Association in 1899. Maybe she met Vincent at an Association meeting? I know very little about Vincent's acting career except for this rather intriguing paragraph in *The Era* of May 13th 1899:

> *"There was no performance at the Cheltenham Opera House on Monday through the non-appearance of Mr Vincent Carlyle's company in Robespierre, which was billed to appear, the performance was stopped by a telegram from Sir Henry Irving's solicitor threatening an action for an injunction if Robespierre was played."*

Henry Irving was arguably the most influential actor/manager of the Victorian period, being the first thespian ever to be knighted. He had opened at the Lyceum Theatre, London with Robespierre in April 1899 after recovering from a serious illness. Presumably he owned the right to the play and Carlyle was attempting to piggyback on the popularity of the London production and was promptly stopped by the threat of legal action.

Vincent served as a Lance Corporal in the 6th Battalion of King's Royal Rifles Corp during the first world war; the 5th and 6th battalions of the KRRC being reservists who remained stationed in the UK throughout the duration. He was awarded the Silver War Badge, which was issued in the UK to service personnel who had been honourably discharged due to wounds or sickness during the First World War. It was first issued in 1916 along with a certificate and the badge was intended to be worn on civilian clothes. There was a practice amongst some women during the war to present apparently able-bodied young men with white feathers, shaming them for their cowardice in not wearing a uniform and fighting for King and country. The silver badge was an attempt to avoid this humiliation when there was a legitimate reason for them not to be in uniform.

I can find no trace of Lillian in newspaper ads after the spring of 1917 when, ironically, she was touring with a play called 'The Girl Who Wouldn't Marry', until in November 1922 she appears at the Royal Theatre in Bristol, playing in 'His Child Wife'. It's possible that she changed her name again during this period but I can find nothing listed under any combination of her first names and Carlyle. The 1922 mention is the last appearance I can trace until her death in 1925.

Lily Blanche Rainbow otherwise Herries died on 12th August 1925 at the National Hospital, Queen Square, Holborn, London. Her age is given as 56 and her address is 3, Albert Street, Newcastle under Lyme. She is recorded as the actress daughter of John Rainbow (deceased) Theatre Proprietor. The cause of death was Amyotrophic Lateral Sclerosis, Bulbar Palsy - this particularly cruel illness is more commonly known as Motor Neurone Disease in the UK (the same disease Stephen Hawking suffers from) and Lou Gehrig's disease in the USA. It seems particularly poignant that this disease, which robs the sufferer of speech and mobility in such an aggressive manner, should afflict an actress whose reviews were often focused on her physical attributes; her daintiness, prettiness and her perfect elocution. Even more affecting if she had been abandoned, in this time of need, by her husband and friends. I have not been able to find an obituary in The Stage or any other national or provincial newspaper.

As mentioned earlier the informant of personal details on the death certificate was her cousin, Harry Aynsleigh who lived in Dagenham, Essex and its probably safe to say he got Lillie's age wrong as well as the name of her father and her marital status. I can find no record of a divorce from Vincent and he didn't pre-decease her. As far as I am able to establish I can find no trace of a will.

Chasing Rainbows

VICTORIANS AND EDWARDIANS

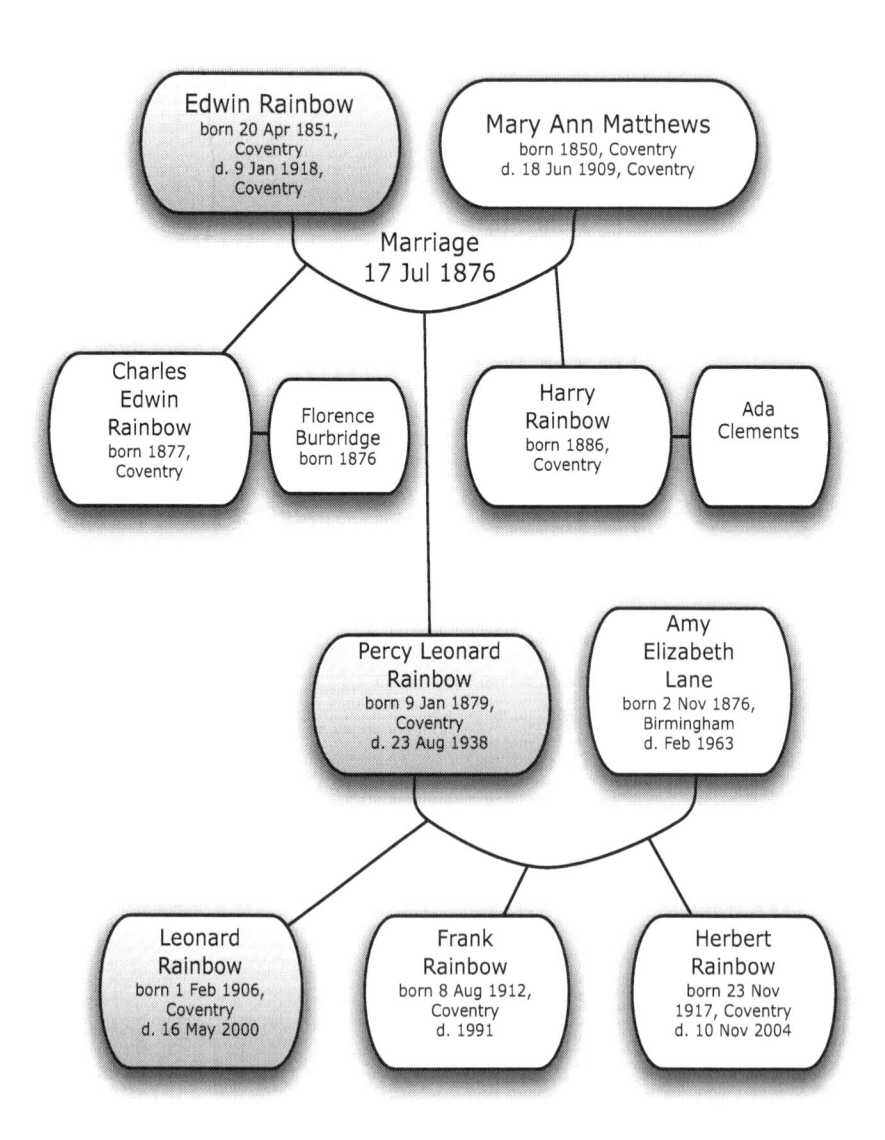

Edwin Rainbow
born 20 Apr 1851, Coventry
d. 9 Jan 1918, Coventry

Mary Ann Matthews
born 1850, Coventry
d. 18 Jun 1909, Coventry

Marriage 17 Jul 1876

Charles Edwin Rainbow
born 1877, Coventry

Florence Burbridge
born 1876

Harry Rainbow
born 1886, Coventry

Ada Clements

Percy Leonard Rainbow
born 9 Jan 1879, Coventry
d. 23 Aug 1938

Amy Elizabeth Lane
born 2 Nov 1876, Birmingham
d. Feb 1963

Leonard Rainbow
born 1 Feb 1906, Coventry
d. 16 May 2000

Frank Rainbow
born 8 Aug 1912, Coventry
d. 1991

Herbert Rainbow
born 23 Nov 1917, Coventry
d. 10 Nov 2004

Edwin Rainbow

Edwin Rainbow was born on 20th April 1851 in High Street, Coventry. His parents were James Rainbow and Sarah (nee Hinton) who were both 41 at the time of his birth.

This photo of Edwin, (above) the kindly looking old gentleman who resembled my grandad, Len, was another source of inspiration to me to research the family history. I wanted to know more about him. The photo would have been taken near to the end of his life and was given to me by Len when I was a young woman. I'm 99% certain that this is Edwin because Len was very close to him and he gave it to me when I first started researching the family tree, back in the early 1980s. Len was mentally sound and this was his only and treasured photo of his granddad.

Chasing Rainbows

I make this point because several years ago, Linda Jeffs, the daughter of Herbert Rainbow and Len's niece, kindly passed me the photo (below) that she had found amongst her father's possessions after his death. Herbert had told her that this was a photo of Edwin.

This involves us in a mystery, as I don't believe its possible that both photos can be of Edwin. The second photo appears to be of a much older man and yet he has more hair than the Edwin in the first photo. If it's not a wig they can't both be Edwin! However there is a strong family resemblance and, in fact, they both share a resemblance to Len at different times of his life. I realised after checking dates that Herbert wasn't born until November 1917 and was only a few weeks old when Edwin died early in 1918, so he wouldn't have had any actual memory of his granddad. Len, on the other hand was born in 1906 and had a close relationship with this grandfather, living with him for at least 10 years before his death. Given all this evidence I'm certain that the second photo is not Edwin and I would suggest that it might be Edwin's father, James Rainbow. James died in 1883 aged 73 so it is perfectly possible that a photo was taken in the years leading up to his death. However, there is a fly in the genealogical ointment, the clothes that he's wearing seem to suggest a later period of time - turn ups on trousers were popularised by King Edward, as late as the first decade of the twentieth century. In that case I could be completely wrong and it may be someone else altogether, maybe one of Edwin's older brothers.

Edwin attended Bablake (pronounced bab-lick) School. In recent times and certainly since my childhood Bablake was the 'posh' school, the independent school for fee payers, but that hadn't always been the case. Black's Warwickshire guide of 1866 (Black Adam and Charles, Ltd) gives a brief overview of the school, its history and structure:

> "The school was founded in 1560 by Thomas Wheatley, mayor of Coventry. It is devoted to the education of about fifty boys for a period of two years each. The boys are partially provided for the first year, and wholly for the second; and, on leaving, are apprenticed for seven years to such trades as their parents or friends may choose for them."

In fact, it is believed that the school is much older and dates to the fourteenth century, making it one of the oldest schools in England. Queen Isabella, the widow of Edward II donated a piece of land to build the original St. John's Church, sometimes known as Bablake church and it was believed that Bablake School was established by 1364. In an 1832 edition of the newspaper, *John Bull* there includes a description of how Bablake came to be endowed as a charity school:

> "Part of Bablake Hospital at Coventry is appropriated for the residence of a number of poor boys, on a foundation instituted by Thomas Wheatley, Mayor, ironmonger and wool-cardmaker, in consequence of the following singular incident: - Having sent his servant to Spain in 1556, to purchase barrels of steel gads, or ingots, he bought, by some inexplicable mistake, and brought home, a number of casks filled with ingots of silver and cochineal, which were offered for sale in an open fair, as the articles he was directed to purchase. His worthy master made

> *afterwards every effort to discover the person who sold them, but ineffectually and finally converted the whole value, together with all his property, to the establishment of this charity."*

This unforeseen good fortune was put to good use by Bablake School and provided education, free board and clothing to needy boys who, ultimately, went on to become apprentices. At the time that Edwin went to Bablake it was a charity school and, after leaving school, Edwin became an apprentice printer. He served his seven-year apprenticeship at the office of *The Coventry Standard* and once his term was finished found employment with *The Coventry Times*, where he became a printer's reader, what we would now call a proofreader, before turning to journalism.

On 17th July 1876 Edwin married Mary Ann Matthews, and they had three boys Charles Edwin, Percy Leonard and Harry. Mary was the daughter of John and Mary Ann Matthews (nee Booth), both were listed as silk weavers.

There is a lot of information from various sources about Edwin floating around but tantalisingly it always seems to fall short of the full story. He was active in his community as a journalist and later was appointed Registrar of Births & Deaths in Coventry. His signature turns up on many birth and death certificates and he registered Len's birth. He was involved with the Coventry School of Arts and the Technical College being appointed Secretary of both these institutions at various times. [7]

In these days of polarisation it was interesting to discover that Edwin was both a religious man and interested in scientific discoveries and advancements. He was a prominent member of his local Baptist Church and yet also helped organise scientific lectures. He taught at adult education classes, being particularly interested in vocational education to improve the business prospects of the area, he was concerned that superior training in Europe was leading to Britain being left behind.

---

[7]   see appendix

Edwin's childhood must have been filled with turmoil and poverty. He was the youngest son of relatively poor silk weavers going through an economic slump so severe that his father left the family home to work as a servant for his aunt. Soup kitchens were made available to silk weavers and his father's younger brother and family shared their home. Not surprising then, that when he achieved some measure of affluence and influence, he was eager to encourage anything that might aid and support the development of industry in the town. He learnt, taught and supervised exams in shorthand when it was cutting edge. In 1877 he was elected to the Newspaper Press Fund, the journalist's charity and in 1897 he was appointed special local secretary to superintend examinations at the Department of Science and Art.

He wrote about his wish that Coventry should have a museum to record the development of local trades including the silk weaving industry. I was acutely aware of this when visiting the Herbert Art Gallery and Museum in Coventry and Huw Jones, Keeper of Industry, showed me examples of silk weaving from the 19th century and the exhibition tracing the development of the trade in the city.

In the early days of the twentieth century Edwin visited Bohemia (a country that equates roughly to the modern Czech Republic) and began his love affair with that part of the world, writing articles about his travels in order to finance his trips.

There is one mystery surrounding Edwin that I haven't been able to solve. In one of his obituaries it was mentioned that he became less prominent in local journalism due to 'circumstances' in 1895. I have yet to discover what these circumstances may have been. He was still active in journalism, as one of his trips to Bohemia with a deputation from the British Institute of Journalists was in 1905 and I believe he wrote travel articles for national newspapers, including The Guardian. It's difficult to ascertain this information as journalists didn't get a byline and most articles were attributed to 'our own correspondent'. I can't find any documented personal reasons for his withdrawal from local journalism and we can only speculate that there may have been some dispute with his employer and/or the newspaper proprietor.

Another snippet of information I remember from Len was that when Edwin was in Bohemia he became friendly with a man called Mr Musek who Len remembered coming to Coventry for a return visit. I've no idea who Mr Musek might have been, although some superficial research has discovered Pan Karel Musek (1867-1924), actor and stage manager of the Royal Bohemian National Theatre in Prague who in the summer of 1905 was translating a John Millington Synge play into Czech. Could he also have been acting as a translator for a British deputation of journalists? On the face of it this would seem a superficial task for a theatre manager, but the deputation was important enough that at least one of the party was awarded the freedom of Prague for their services with regard to the dissemination of information about Bohemia. This is, however, pure speculation on my part.

Edwin's obituaries[8] are interesting in respect of one appearing in a local paper and a few days later a response was published that felt that the original 'writer of the memoir' hadn't done him full justice. One cannot help speculating that there may have been some friction between people who were likely to be former colleagues or friends.

Aside from the facts and figures and on a more personal note, I remember as a child and later as an adult being told about Edwin by Len. He was very proud of his granddad and they had a close relationship. I know Len was deeply affected by Edwin's sudden death at the age of 66 and he very much regretted that his granddad, who despised the war, died before it ended in 1918.

In 2002 the *Coventry Evening Telegraph* published an account of Edwin's life as told by his granddaughter, Barbara Dey of Lupton Avenue, Coventry to David McGrory in his 'Weekend Time Tunnel' column. Barbara was the daughter of Harry Rainbow, Edwin's youngest son and Ada (nee Clements). The article begins by repeating the family story that the Rainbows were descended from Huguenots fleeing from France and that John Rainbow, b. 1746 in Lutterworth

---

8   see appendix

was the son of James Rainbow, a silk weaver from Spittalfields in London.

As previously mentioned the parish records that I have discovered reveal that although John was baptised in Lutterworth he was born in the village of Cotesbach and was the son of William Rainbow and Phoebe Taylor. I'm intrigued by the mention of James though and wonder if he could be William's father. More work is needed in that area. The article goes on to describe Edwin's life working for the Coventry Herald, owned by Charles Bray and that "his work and pleasant style brought him to prominence, entertaining and informing readers in both Birmingham and London newspapers". He authored and edited several books including the official guide accompanying Queen Victoria's Jubilee celebrations and a local travel guide 'Walks Thru' Coventry' (a copy of which I have in my possession). He joined the Institute of Journalists in 1887 and he was a member and deputy chairman of the Birmingham and Midland district committee of the Institute of Journalists until shortly before his death.

According to Barbara he attended many meetings and it was during this time, after he married Mary Ann that he took his first trip to Prague, which was then in Bohemia and they both fell in love with the country. At that time Bohemia was getting bad press in Europe initiated by Germany and Edwin was a welcome visitor as he wrote positive articles about the people of Bohemia and his trips that were published in English national newspapers. He also gave both public and private talks about Bohemia and was commended in the Bohemian press for his "true friendship". The Coventry Evening Telegraph article quotes a Bohemian newspaper of 1911, " his [Edwin's] articles about Prague and Bohemia showed his English readers quite a different picture from the one they were accustomed to from the German newspapers."

When Mary died in 1909, flowers were sent to her funeral from Prague.

In a rare honour for a foreign journalist Edwin was awarded a silver medal, a certificate of merit and Freedom of the City of Prague for his services as a journalist. I believe that the medal and certificate were in the possession of Barbara Dey at the time the article was written in 2002.

Edwin died suddenly on 9th January 1918 and was buried in Coventry Cemetery on Saturday 12th January.

The probate office records his will as follows:

> *Rainbow, Edwin of 30 Queen's Road, Coventry journalist died 9 January 1918 Probate Birmingham 7 February to Charles Edwin Rainbow chartered secretary Percy Leonard Rainbow carpenter and joiner and Harry Rainbow commercial clerk. Effects £2857 11s 4d. Resworn £3097 11s 4d.*

This would be the equivalent of approximately £63,000 at the time of writing (2010).

His memoriam card reads:

"One clear call for me"

Died on 9th January 1918 at 30, Queen's Road, Coventry. Edwin Rainbow, the Father of Charles Edwin, Percy Leonard and Harry Rainbow. Aged 66 years.

"The last end

Of the good man is peace! How calm his exit!

Night dews fall not more gently to the ground,

Nor weary worn-out winds expire so soft."

Chasing Rainbows

HENRY RAINBOW AND FAMILY

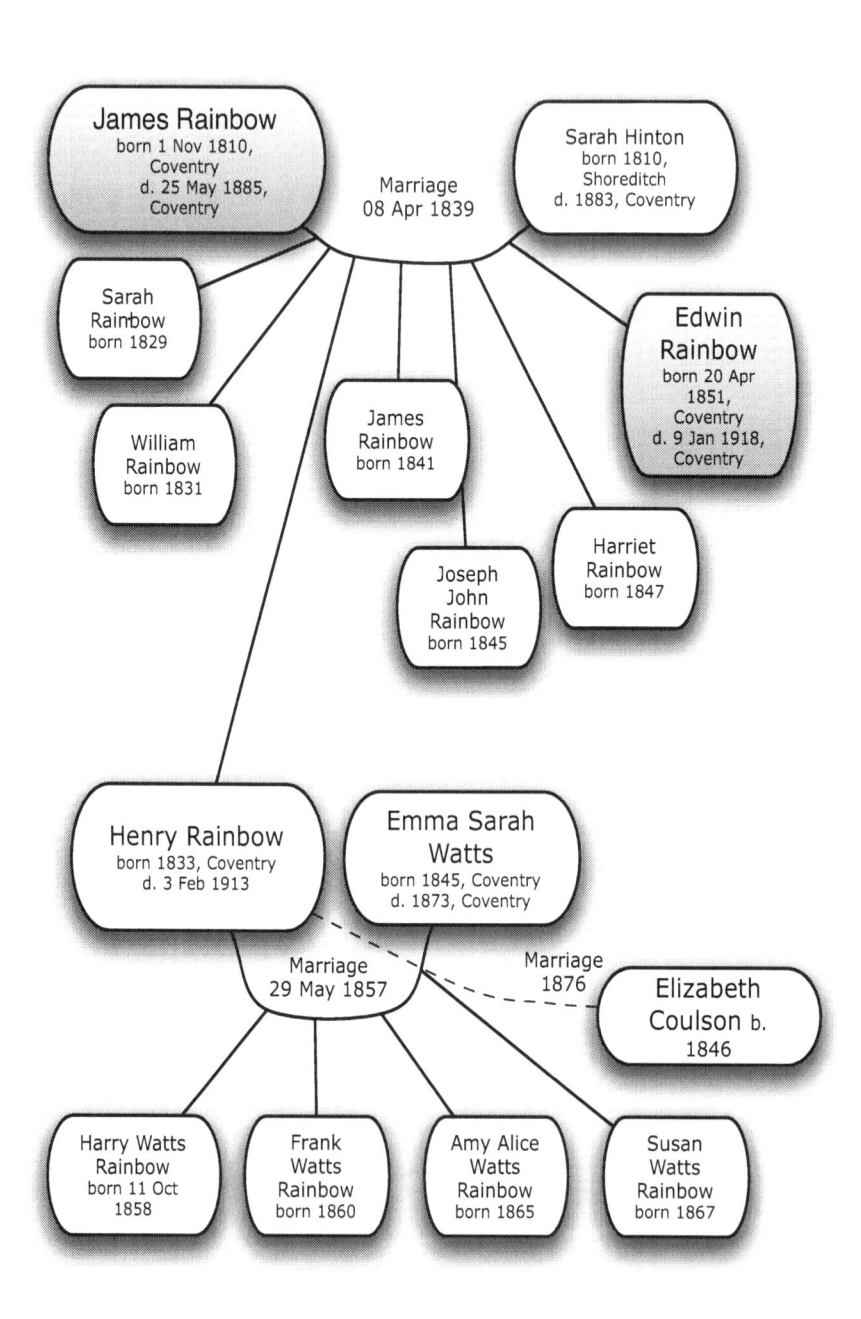

James Rainbow
born 1 Nov 1810, Coventry
d. 25 May 1885, Coventry

Marriage 08 Apr 1839

Sarah Hinton
born 1810, Shoreditch
d. 1883, Coventry

Sarah Rainbow
born 1829

William Rainbow
born 1831

James Rainbow
born 1841

Joseph John Rainbow
born 1845

Harriet Rainbow
born 1847

Edwin Rainbow
born 20 Apr 1851, Coventry
d. 9 Jan 1918, Coventry

Henry Rainbow
born 1833, Coventry
d. 3 Feb 1913

Emma Sarah Watts
born 1845, Coventry
d. 1873, Coventry

Marriage 29 May 1857

Marriage 1876

Elizabeth Coulson b. 1846

Harry Watts Rainbow
born 11 Oct 1858

Frank Watts Rainbow
born 1860

Amy Alice Watts Rainbow
born 1865

Susan Watts Rainbow
born 1867

142

Henry Rainbow

Henry Rainbow must have been a serious man. In his obituary [9] written by his pastor he was described as a

> "solid, quiet character without ostentation... a grave, practical, matter of fact man." The pastor went so far to say " No winds of passion, nor tremors of excitement were seen in him. Equable, patient, self possessed...he was the very personification of uprightness, integrity and common sense. Perhaps a little of the emotional and fervent would have given him a richer tone to his life..."

Reading between the lines he must have been a dour character for a Victorian pastor to make such a comment!

Henry was the second son of James and Sarah, born in Coventry in 1833. His original occupation was as a silk weaver and this is listed as his trade in three census returns from 1851 through to 1871. On 29th May 1857 he married Emma Sarah Watts and they had four children, Harry Watts Rainbow (1858), Frank Watts Rainbow (1860), Amy Alice Watts Rainbow (1865) and Susan S. Watts Rainbow (1867).

In 1873 Emma died aged 40, leaving Henry with four children to raise. Three years later Henry married his first cousin, Elizabeth Coulson, the daughter of his father's sister, also Elizabeth (nee Rainbow). His new bride was eleven years his junior and they were to have no children. The following year, 1877, Henry's eldest son, Harry died of heart disease at the age of eighteen. By this time Henry was no longer a silk worker, he was listed as a refreshment housekeeper living at 3 and 4 Market Street, Coventry. At the time of the 1881 census he was living there with Elizabeth and the three children. Frank was listed as a brewer's clerk and Amy Alice was a 'pupil teacher'. They have a lodger and a servant.

---

9 (see appendix)

In 1891 Henry and Elizabeth were still at Market Street with Frank promoted to 'refreshment house keeper (assistant)' and Amy Alice a schoolteacher.

By the time of the 1901 census Henry had handed over the business to his son Frank and retired to 1, Lincoln Street. He was living there with Elizabeth and Amy Alice who was now an 'Assistant School Mistress' (a demotion?)

One of the stories that my granddad Len told me was that when he was a child Edwin would take him into Coventry town centre and one of the favourite places to stop was 'the cooked ham shop owned by Edwin's brother'. I can't find any trace of this establishment in the records but from what Len said it was in Market Street and I'm wondering if, by that time, (around 1912-18) they had either turned the restaurant into a cold meat shop or it was now dual purpose. Len appeared to have strong memories of this being a pleasant experience but the question is, who was the 'brother'? Could it have been Henry, just before his death in 1913?

Henry had retired by 1901 and handed over to Frank, but Frank died in 1902 of cirrhosis of the liver. Frank never married and he didn't leave a will. It may be that Henry still held ownership of the business even though he'd retired to let Frank run it. Speculation: Frank had a drink problem and Henry wanted to retain control?

Henry died in February 1913 at the age of 80 and with all the trauma in his life it may not be too surprising that he appeared to be on the serious side.

At this point I haven't seen details of Henry's will but I do know that he left £3,814 (a substantial sum of money in 1913), which was to be shared between Amy Alice and Edwin - his daughter and his brother, with nothing to his wife!

Amy Alice Watts Rainbow

Amy Alice Watts Rainbow was the daughter of Henry Rainbow and niece of Edwin. She never married and she worked as a schoolteacher. I have seen her signature on several civil registration certificates and I believe that she deputised for Edwin as a registrar of births and deaths, maybe when he was away on trips to Bohemia and she certainly signed Edwin's own certificate after his sudden death, so presumably she had the authority to take his place. I've seen her referred to as Alice both on certificates and in a letter sent from a Henry Rainbow, New York in 1983 in response to a genealogical enquiry that has subsequently been passed around various family members. In the letter Henry refers to the research and attached family tree completed by 'Aunt Alice' who I believe must be Amy Alice Watts Rainbow. This research had been completed years earlier and sent to Henry by his Aunt Olive.

The letter refers generally to the family history, repeating the French Huguenot story and that the family were thought to be descendants of those refugees that had settled in the Midlands in the early 1700s. He goes on to say that he believes the name Rainbow is from the French surname Rambeau or was adapted from the Rainbow Tavern, where the Huguenot's gathered in London. He also mentions a connection with the Bishop of Carlisle, Edward Rainbow. All of these facts could be based on research or pure speculation, and as mentioned earlier I have not been able to prove or disprove any of them.

What is interesting about the handwritten family tree is that Jabez Rainbow is included with both his birth date and the year of his death. So although the story wasn't common knowledge in the family there must have been some sharing of information; someone must have let the family know that he'd died or a generation further down someone had researched 'Uncle Jabez.' Jabez's date of death was recorded in the Tasmanian archives but would not have been available in Britain,

Chasing Rainbows

at that time, which means that Alice must have known he died in Tasmania and presumably also the reason why he was there. There are no more details on the family tree so I'm assuming that this was to be kept quiet.

Apart from the census information I know very little about AAW Rainbow except that she donated a few pieces of artwork to the Coventry Museum including an engraving of the Coventry Cross by J. Seago, given in 1931. Amy Alice Rainbow died in 1942.

William Ballard RAINBOW

Genfile

Profile

In brief
William Ballard Rainbow, druggist, born 1862, parents William Rainbow and Emma (Ballard). Died 1935

Known for...
his role as Coventry councillor and for his involvement in the Passive Resistance movement.

Events

Year	
1904	He was issued a summons for non-payment of rates - his protest as part of the Coventry and District Passive Resistance League.
1912	William was a founder member The London Road Allotments Ltd.
1935	He died aged 72, a victim of an accident. He was knocked down by a motor van while crossing the road at night and suffered a compound fracture of the skull.

William Ballard Rainbow

William Ballard Rainbow; chemist, Coventry City councillor, founder member of the Coventry Allotment Society, member of the Ratepayer's Association and Passive Resister.

William was born in Coventry in 1862, the son of William Rainbow and Emma (nee Ballard), grandson of James and Sarah. The eldest of three children, in 1881 he appeared in the census as a chemist's apprentice and spent most of his adult life owning and running a chemist and household goods shop as well as holding various public offices in the community.

In 1891 and 1901 he was listed as a dry salter and shopkeeper situated at 115 Gosford Street. Drysalters were dealers in a range of chemical products including glue, varnish, dye and colourings. They also supplied salt or chemicals for preserving food and sometimes sold pickles, dried meat or related items as well as household requisites such as wallpaper paste, bleach, soap, paint and varnish, glycerine, gum arabic, saltpetre, French chalk and raw soap.

In 1911 he was listed in the census as a druggist, living and working at 10, Cash's Lane, Coventry. He was married to Elizabeth (nee Barr) and they were living with their three children, Dorothy aged 19, a pianoforte teacher, Olive Edith, aged 10 and Henry, aged 9. They had a servant, 22 year old Harriet Allen and William's mother, Emma, was living with them. Emma was 80 years old and a widow. The 1911 census returns were not bound by the 100 year closure rule and were released a little early, in 2006, but sensitive information was to be kept locked for the full 100 years. In practice this has meant that, at the time of writing, the last column of the 1911 census returns have been blocked out to hide sensitive information such as hearing and sight disabilities or conditions termed, at the beginning of the 20th century, as 'lunatic' or 'feeble-minded'. On the census return for William and his family, although the last column is not visible it is possible to see that next to Emma's entry is written the word 'Totally...' meaning that she was either totally deaf or totally blind. A look back at the 1901 census reveals that she was blind, although this would appear to be an age onset disability, as the earlier censuses make no mention of it.

William Ballard Rainbow was a Passive Resister. The Passive Resistance movement grew out of the controversial Education Act that was enacted in 1902. It abolished the 2,568 school boards set up by the Elementary Education Act of 1870 and all the School Attendance Committees. The duties and powers were passed to local borough or county councils; the LEAs (local education authorities) were established and given the power to establish new secondary and technical schools as well as building on and developing the existing primary education system. The previously church funded denominational schools were now brought under the control of the government and the LEAs contributed to the costs of all non-religious education in these church schools. The Conservative party, who held power in the government, favoured the church schools and were concerned about the secular education available in state schools and this legislation was seen as an attempt to redress the balance. As by far the biggest proportion of church schools were Anglican, non-conformists complained that it was unfair that Anglican religious education, with which they disagreed, should be paid for out of their taxes.

This was not the first time that the non-conformists had felt aggrieved. They had been forced to pay taxes to contribute to the maintenance of Anglican churches and they were also excluded from holding any military or civil office and barred from being awarded degrees from Oxford and Cambridge.

Protests came from the Liberal party, the Labour movement and the non-conformists. The Baptist leader, John Clifford, formed the National Passive Resistance Movement and "passive resisters" stopped paying the portion of their rates that they deemed to be used for supporting church schools. By the time of the General Election in 1906 more than 170 men had been jailed for their refusal to pay their rates in full but the Conservatives held firm and refused to repeal the law, resulting in the Passive Resistance issue becoming a major contributing issue in the downfall of the Conservative government and the landslide victory by the Liberal party. During the first decade of the 20th century there were several references to the activities of the Coventry and District Passive Resistance League in the local newspapers.

On March 4th 1904, the Coventry Herald reported that over 70 summonses had been served on members of the Passive Resistance movement in the Coventry district for non-payment of rates. The defendants included several non-conformist ministers, town councillors, a Guardian of the Poor, a solicitor and a magistrate. The court was crowded with defendants having to sit in the public gallery, grouped together down the sides of the court and some even having to remain outside in the waiting room. A list was read of those refusing to pay a portion of their rates and the amount owed. Included on this list was William Ballard Rainbow, 5 Victoria Street who owed 2s 6d. As far as I am able to establish William did not have his goods seized or go to jail. The amount he owed appeared to have been paid by an anonymous benefactor before things became too serious.

The non-conformists of the last century felt that the Anglican Church was persecuting them although the Rev. William Blomfield in a letter to the Coventry Herald gave a broader warning of church and state involvement

> *"..what we are now experiencing is simply the latest of the persecuting spirit which has always existed in the Established Church. Persecution is not peculiar to the Anglican Church; it is a necessary adjunct of the establishment. Connect any church, Presbyterian, Methodist or Congregational with the State and it is certain to be intolerant..."*

On January 15th 1905 the Coventry Herald announced:

> *"We have received the following communication from the Coventry and District Passive Resistance League:-*

> *With respect to the current local rate, the members of the above league have unanimously decided to deduct a sum equal to 2d in the £, this being in their opinion that portion of the rate which will be devoted to the support of denominational schools."*

The article went on to give details of a 'limelight lecture' presented by Rev. W.H. Higgins at Gosford Street Chapel. The lecture consisted of a history of passive resistance and its effectiveness throughout the centuries. Photographs were shown both of the protestors and of the sales of their goods that had been seized for non-payment. Rev. Higgins threatened that if the iniquitous law persisted it would not be long before active resistance followed passive. The lecture proved to be popular. The lantern slide equipment was lent by the editor of The Crusader, the newspaper of the Passive Resistance movement. Mr Lloyd manipulated the lantern and Mr Noble presided at the organ.

The law regarding the state funding of church schools was never repealed and it is still contentious today over 100 years later. In the New Statesman, September 2010 in response to an article about the Pope's visit to the UK, a commentator states, "We now have 2,300 Catholic faith schools funded by the tax payer, being allowed to influence the young… diminishing science teaching, preventing our progress toward a fairer society." And so it goes on.

As well as being involved with the Passive Resistance, William was a vocal member of the City Council. On one occasion he seemed concerned that the amount of work he put into council affairs was not truly represented by local newspapers.

The Coventry Herald reports that Mr Rainbow "proceeded to make a vigorous attack on the local Press.:

> *"Ratepayers, he said could not form a strictly accurate idea from newspaper reports. The alderman's speeches were always reported at very great length, and the Mayor's was too: but the ordinary councillor did not get much space. It was a funny little way the newspapers had got;*

he could not explain it. Newspaper reports did not give a good idea as regarded the time representatives put into their work. A few months ago he raised a discussion in regard to the wages paid to brickyard labourers. He got about four lines in the newspapers and that represented four hours hard work.

Councillor Copson: Not in the Council.

Councillor Rainbow said the time was spent in going round to see people. Continuing, he said, he had also spoken upon the question of rating values. The Coventry Herald gave him 52 lines - a very good report - (one cannot help but summon an image of the councillor poring over the newspaper every evening counting how many lines he'd been given) but another paper did not mention a word about it. ("Shame"). The papers seemed to go against them because they were Ratepayers Association representatives."

It is interesting to consider this in the light of the family's involvement with the newspaper industry in Coventry. Edwin, William Ballard's uncle, had worked for various newspapers in the city for approaching forty years. There was the question of the 'circumstances' in 1895 that led to Edwin contributing less to local newspapers. I have not been able to discover what these circumstances were but maybe if there had been a disagreement/scandal it had led to a dislike of certain newspapers and this permeated throughout the family. Alternatively maybe Edwin and William B. disliked each other and William enjoyed taking pot shots at the industry that employed his uncle.

In 1911, together with Joseph Raven, John Trindle and Henry Louis Curzons, William approached Coventry Corporation with a request to obtain land for the provision of allotments. This was not the first involvement of the Rainbows and Curzons; William's great grandfather, Joseph had married Kitty Curzons after the death of his first wife. The London Road Allotments Limited was formed in 1912 and William was elected as Secretary, a position he held for over twenty years, up until his death.

William died in 1935 aged 72 and I discovered, from the Coventry Allotment Society website, that he was the victim of a tragic accident.

His death certificate states that the cause of death was 'laceration of brain due to compound fracture of the skull caused by being knocked down by a motor van while crossing the road at night.'

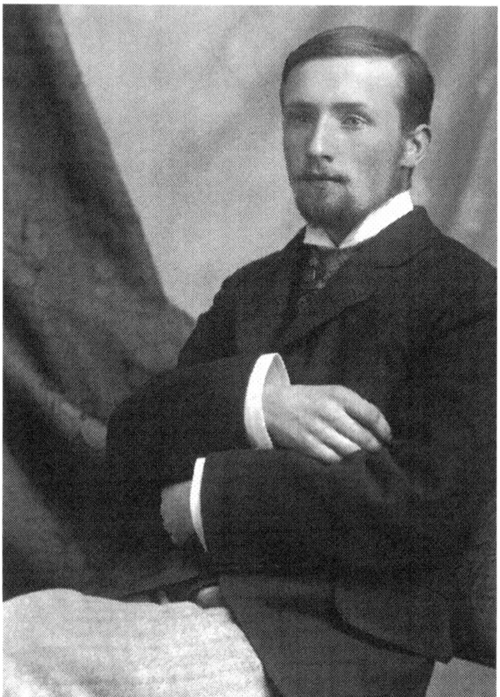

Percy Rainbow

Percy Rainbow, son of Edwin and beloved father of Leonard, was born in 1879 and died in 1938. Apart from the factual birth, marriage and death information most of the information I know about Percy has been gleaned from snippets of information passed on by various members of the family who knew him when he was alive.

Thanks to Linda Jeffs, Percy's granddaughter, there are a few documents remaining that give us an insight into his life, for example he kept his examination certificates from school, the results being:

- Practical Plane and Solid Geometry 30th April 1892, aged 13, Second Class
- Inorganic Chemistry (Theoretical) 14th May 1891, aged 12, Second Class
- Inorganic Chemistry (Practical) 9th and 30th May 1891, aged12, Second Class
- Sound, Light and Heat, 17th May 1892, aged 13, Second Class
- Perspective, 29th April 1892, aged13, First Class
- Geometrical Drawing, 25th April, 1891, Passed

After leaving school he became an apprentice carpenter and little is known about his life from then until his wedding.

Percy married Amy on April 6th 1904. He was 24 and she was 26. On the wedding certificate Percy is listed as a master carpenter and joiner, a bachelor living at 30 Queen's Road, Coventry, Warwickshire, England; his father is Edwin Rainbow, journalist. Amy Elizabeth Lane is listed as a spinster living at 57, Fontenoy Street, Dublin, her father is Mathew (sic) Henry Lane, brass finisher. Percy and Amy were married at Philsborough Baptist Church in Dublin, Ireland.

Amy was born in the Ladywood area of Birmingham on 11th February 1877 but by the time of the 1881 census was living with her family, father Henry and mother Priscilla in Castle Street, Coventry along with her brothers Thomas, aged 7, Jabez aged 4 months and stepbrother William Berwick Jackson (Priscilla's son from a previous relationship).

As an aside Priscilla's maiden name was Berwick and, at the time of writing, my mother, Patricia Sanders, has in her possession a beautifully hand made wooden sewing box that we believe was made by Percy for his mother-in-law, with the initials PB inlaid in mother of pearl on the outside of the lid. This speculation is based on apocryphal evidence that Percy made the piece and that Priscilla is the only member of the family that had the initials PB, although there is the obvious question as to why he would use her maiden name?

Another family story is that Tommy Lane, Amy's older brother, was a champion jockey in Ireland and although I haven't been able to prove this definitively the records certainly lend some credence to the story, or at least that he was a jockey. My grandfather, Len also told me that his mother, Amy, was 'in-service' to a wealthy family in Ireland.

In 1891 the family had moved to Bradford Street, Coventry. Amy, at 14, was a fancy trimming maker, Jabez was 10 and another younger brother, Hubert F Lane was 4 years old. Thomas, who would have been 17, is not listed on the census with the family but there is a Thomas Lane, aged 17, apprentice to Joseph Cannon, a horse trainer at Clifton House, Newmarket. The rest of this household consists of Joseph's wife Annie, brother-in-law Harry Sharpe - also a horse trainer, the Cannon's three children as well as a cook, a nurse, a housemaid and a kitchen maid. Including Thomas there were nine other apprentices ranging in age from 14 to 18 years. A line has been struck through the birthplace section relating to all ten young men with the addition of the word 'unknown' so we only have the correct name and age to link him with Amy's brother.

However, sometime during the following ten years, the family moved to Ireland. In the 1901 Irish census Henry Lane, brass finisher aged

50 is living with Priscilla, his wife, aged 58 and their daughter Amy Elizabeth aged 24 at 57, Fontenoy Street, Dublin. Amy's occupation is given as a Children's Nurse (written immediately after those words and hard to read, I believe it says, 'unemployed'). All the family's religion is listed as Church of England and their birthplace, England.

Tommy is not on the census and I can't find either Jabez or Hubert, either on the Irish or British census.

Moving forward to the 1911 census and Henry Lane was still living at 57, Fontenoy Street, Dublin but his status is 'boarder' and an English family, the Neils, are the householders. He's listed as Matthew, his occupation remains that of a brass finisher, however Priscilla must have died in the ten years since the 1901 census as his marital status is widower.

Also on the 1911 census, living in Cooldrinagh, Lucan west of Dublin, was Thomas Lane, a jockey, aged 37, who was born in England. This fits in neatly with the information we have but is by no means definitive. Thomas is living with his wife, Margaret and Christy Weldon, listed as brother. It's possible that this has been transcribed in error and should be brother-in-law, which would give Margaret the maiden name of Weldon. They have three children, Margaret 3, Christina 1 and Thomas, 1 month. During the six years of their marriage they have had five children with only these three still living. All the family are listed as Roman Catholics and although Thomas was originally a Protestant it would be a requirement for a would-be groom to convert to Catholicism in order to be married in the Roman Catholic church.

There appears to be some confusion about whether 'our' Tommy Lane could have been a champion jockey. Tommy Lane was indeed famous on the horseracing scene at the turn of the twentieth century and, in fact, he won the French Derby on more than one occasion. However this was "Tommy" Lane, the French jockey. He is described as being French in the newspapers of the time, and when he won the 1891 French Derby 'our' Tommy was still an apprentice jockey in Newmarket. Moreover on Saturday June 13th 1903 *The Racing World* contained an article about the death of 'poor Tommy Lane', one of the 'best finishers in France.' The man I believe to be Amy's brother, 'Thomas Lane, jockey' was alive and living in Dublin in 1911.

One wonders if the story of the famous Tommy Lane got merged in the family because of the coincidence of the name and the story was erroneously handed down that 'Uncle' Tommy was a champion jockey. I may be maligning 'our' Tommy but I can find no record of his racing career.

So the mystery of why the whole family, with the possible exception of Jabez and Hubert, moved to Ireland sometime during the 1890s remains.

The other piece of family information I have about this period is that Len remembered visiting Ireland on more than one occasion as a small child. The childhood memory of that time that particularly stuck in his mind was that he hated the locally made soda bread with a vengeance. In the last few years before he died he regularly visited me when I lived in Co. Mayo, Ireland and it was there that he, reluctantly, tried it again and concluded that it wasn't quite as bad as he'd remembered! He wasn't able to recall at what age he was as a child when visiting Ireland, except that he was very young and he thought the family, Percy, Amy and himself stayed around the Wicklow area. Len seemed to think that this was something to do with his mother being 'in service' and returning to Ireland to visit the family she used to work for. This may well be the case, but it is also possible that she came over to visit her father and/or brother.

One wonders how Percy and Amy met. Was it in Coventry before Amy's family moved to Ireland and they continued the romance at a distance? It is also possible that Percy visited Ireland with his father. Edwin is known to have attended the Journalist's conference in Dublin on at least one occasion during the first few years of the nineteen hundreds. Whatever the circumstances, there is a vague notion that they 'ran away' to get married because the Rainbows didn't approve of the union. Certainly Amy's father was at the wedding as he was named as a witness but there is no clue as to whether Edwin, Mary Ann or either of Percy's brothers attended.

There is also no clue as to whether they stayed in Ireland for a while or just married there. Certainly by the time of the 1911 census they were living in Coventry, six years married with five-year-old Leonard having been born in the city. Percy's career appeared to fluctuate quite markedly over the next few years. According to Len the family lived in Queen Victoria Road after their marriage and Percy ran a carpentry business from a workshop at the rear of the house until 1910, at which time they moved to Edwin's house at Queen's Road, Coventry. I believe his business was struggling at this point. After Edwin's death in 1918 the family moved to 13, Waverley Road and I understand there was some dispute regarding Edwin's will between the three sons. From 1921, Percy and his family lived in Warwick, running a general store in Smith Street; Percy built a cafe at the rear, finally selling to Masons in 1924. From there they moved to Old Square, Warwick before their final move to Emscote Road, Warwick in 1925. After selling the shop Percy went back to the carpentry and building trade, he built several houses included two in Priory Road, Kenilworth. Unfortunately, because of the economic depression in the 1920's he struggled to sell them and that caused some financial hardship for the family.

Len told me that Percy sang in the choir at Queen's Road Baptist church and at various church functions. He apparently had a good baritone voice, which was particularly resounding when he sang 'On the Road to Mandalay'. The family, Percy and his three boys were also involved with the Boy's Brigade in Coventry for many years.

The Boy's Brigade began in Glasgow in 1883, an idea conceived by William Smith. He was concerned that boys and young men were bored and getting into trouble and put together an organisation that combined fun activities with military style drill, all with a strong Christian ethos. The idea spread rapidly and became an international and interdenominational organisation. The Boy's Brigade in Coventry was linked with Queen's Road Baptist Church.

No doubt influenced by his father's interest in further and vocational education Percy tutored in building construction at the local technical college and according to Len during the First World War his father supervised women working in a factory making wooden spars for aeroplanes.

Percy Leonard Rainbow died on 23rd August 1938 at Warneford Hospital, Leamington Spa. He was just 59 years old and died as the result of what should have been a routine operation to repair a hernia. Unfortunately he suffered from a complication of surgery, a post-operative thrombosis and a pulmonary embolism, which proved fatal. His will records that he left £360.10s to his widow, Amy Elizabeth, the equivalent, in 2010, of about £10,000.

20TH CENTURY RAINBOWS

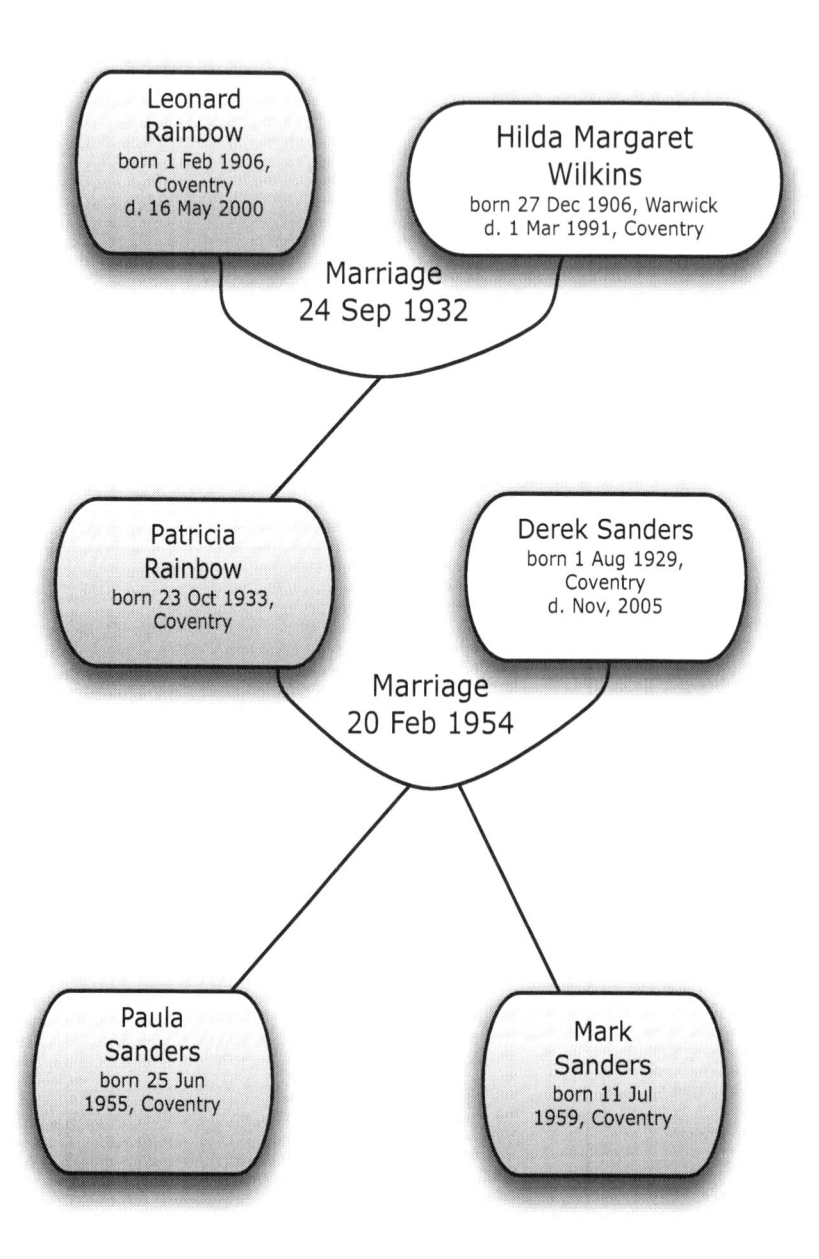

Leonard Rainbow
born 1 Feb 1906, Coventry
d. 16 May 2000

Hilda Margaret Wilkins
born 27 Dec 1906, Warwick
d. 1 Mar 1991, Coventry

Marriage 24 Sep 1932

Patricia Rainbow
born 23 Oct 1933, Coventry

Derek Sanders
born 1 Aug 1929, Coventry
d. Nov, 2005

Marriage 20 Feb 1954

Paula Sanders
born 25 Jun 1955, Coventry

Mark Sanders
born 11 Jul 1959, Coventry

Leonard Rainbow

Leonard Rainbow was born on 1st February 1906 at Queen Victoria Road, Coventry, the eldest child of Percy Rainbow and Amy (nee Lane), although I don't think I ever heard him called Leonard, only by his wife, Hilda, when she was teasing him. It was Len or Pop. He was my grandfather, the only grandfather I had as my dad's father had died shortly before he was born.

The strange thing for me, when writing about Len, is that although we were very close, I know very little about him as a man other than in his role as grandfather.

I know he was close to both his father and grandfather and he was greatly affected by the early death of both. He went to Bablake School as boy and was proud to have been educated at the same school as his grandfather. I believe he had would have liked to go on to university but the funds were not available for more than one son to take this route and it was his younger brother Frank who went on to study for a degree and subsequently became a teacher. When Len left school he went to Wales and worked for W H Smith. At that time he was 'courting' Hilda Wilkins who lived in Warwick. He didn't like being away from home and always associated Wales with bad weather and misery for the rest of his life.

On 24th September 1932, Len and Hilda married at All Saint's Church, Emscote, Warwick and just over a year later, on 23rd October 1933 Hilda gave birth to their only child, Patricia.

During World War II, Len joined the Home Guard. Although those of us brought up in the post-war years will undoubtedly associate these home based soldiers with the television programme *Dad's Army*, this was a force that was formed when there was a real risk of invasion by Germany. When the initial call for volunteers was made in May 1940 the government was expecting 150,000 men to join up and in fact,

Chasing Rainbows

during the first month they received applications from 750,000 men. By the end of June the figure had risen to one million of mainly civilian men who could not join the regular Army because they were either too young, too old or their occupation was considered too important for them to leave. Being a member of the Home Guard was not always easy. The men had to turn out for exercises and manoeuvres, but were unpaid and still had to hold down their normal jobs and support their families.

I haven't been able to establish when Len joined the Home Guard but he must have been in one of the first batches of recruits; he was 33 years old when war broke out so wasn't 'called up' to the regular armed forces initially. My mother believes that he was on Home Guard duty, as an air raid warden, in Coventry on the worst night of the Blitz, 14th November 1940. The rest of the family had left their home in the city by that time and were living with Hilda's mother, Margaret, in Warwick. When Len came home after the German bombers had all but destroyed Coventry he simply said, "You don't want to see our house." A bomb had scored a direct hit and it was completely destroyed.

At the outset of war, in 1939, only young men were conscripted; for the first 6 months only those aged 18-21, but as the war progressed the armed forces reached out to older and older age groups. Len was around 38 when he was called up in 1944 and he joined the RAF as part of the ground maintenance crew. He was sent out to Iraq as part of 40 Staging Post.

RAF Habbaniya was situated on the banks of the Euphrates River in Iraq, about 55 miles from Baghdad and was opened in 1936. By any standards it was an unusual place as Len wrote in a letter to Pat.[10]

> *"It's really a very nice camp and far better than any I have heard of in England. There is also a big swimming pool, which is opening next week! I think!! So I shall be able to have a swim and keep cool."*

---
10 full text of letters see appendix

The swimming pool in question was no grubby little splash bath for keeping troops cool in the 100F degrees plus temperatures but a full Olympic sized swimming pool, just one of a number of leisure facilities one might think more associated with a luxury hotel than a wartime military camp.

Habbaniya was the jewel in the crown of military camps, an oasis in the desert complete with tree-lined road, lawns and flower gardens courtesy of an irrigation system using water piped from the Euphrates. The size of a small town, it was enclosed with a perimeter fence that was 7 miles long and 10 feet high. As well as military personnel it was also home to 10,000 civilians who lived in the Civil Cantonment area of the camp - a town within a town. This population included civilian workers and displaced people of the region. After the First World War there were many people who had fought against the Russians and Ottomans and who came under the protection of the British when peace was restored. Many different cultures, races and religions came together at Habbaniya including Indians, Armenians, Persians, Assyrians and Kurds.

The camp was of such a size that the RAF housed a division of mounted police and parades were often reviewed on horseback. Incredibly Habbaniya even had its own hunt. The Royal Exodus Hunt had a pack of fox hounds, a Master of the Hunt, mounted riders and they would hunt jackal and foxes in the desert around the perimeter of the camp.

Of course, even though this was a relatively luxurious camp by military standards nothing could compensate for being away from home and family and Len's letters home are poignantly strewn with lines such as, 'it won't be long now', and 'what fun we'll have when I come home.'

After the war Len worked as an insurance agent for the Prudential Assurance Company, a job he held until his retirement. This was in the days when the 'insurance man' would call round weekly to collect the premiums for life insurance. I remember as a young child sitting at the wooden 'bureau' in Len and Hilda's back bedroom and 'helping' with his accounts which consisted mainly of playing with the coins that he tipped out of his leather collecting bag and stacking the half crowns into piles of eight. At that time the whole family were living in Buckingham Rise, Allesley Park, Coventry. Hilda and Len lived in the upper maisonette, number twenty-eight and my Mum, Dad, me and later my brother, Mark lived underneath at number twenty-six.

In the early sixties a family decision was made to sell both maisonettes and buy a house jointly in Devon, a favourite holiday haunt. A house was bought and the family moved down, except for Len who continued with his job at the Prudential counting off the months until he could take early retirement, in the interim commuting down to Devon whenever he could. Finally in 1966 he retired. He was very proud of being invited to London with Hilda to the Prudential head office for a presentation, which included a stay in a nice hotel and a fancy dinner.

With retirement came a little more money and Len purchased a static caravan at a holiday park in nearby Paignton. Mark and I spent most of our summer holidays for the next few years "up at the van."

The Devon years, as I mentioned earlier, were a mixed bag of rural idyll and family conflict. Ultimately, in the winter of 1970/71 my parents decided to move back to Coventry and the house was sold; Len and Hilda bought a small bungalow in Brixham and my parents moved in with my Uncle Maurice (Mol) until they were allocated social housing.

I think the financial problems that beset Len's father particularly through the depression years affected the way he handled finances throughout the rest of his life giving him a reputation of being 'careful' with money. However, his motivation for being cautious was largely driven by the desire to leave a generous inheritance to his daughter and grandchildren after his death and his careful attitude to spending money never prohibited him from helping out family with gifts of cash when they were going through difficulties.

Patricia Rainbow

This is the only living person I've included and was written, with her permission, after I'd interviewed Patricia, my mum, towards the end of 2010.

Patricia Rainbow was born on 23rd October 1933, the only child of Len and Hilda Rainbow, at Wheatley Street, Coventry. Len had bought the house after he had returned from working for W.H. Smith in Wales, married Hilda and started working for the Prudential.

Pat remembers that there was no electricity at the house and they only had an outside toilet, which was not unusual for that period. It was a two up, two down and you walked straight from the street into the living room. When she was about five she went to Wheatley Street School and felt like an outsider, partly due to being an only child and partly due to her father having a white collar job which would have been different to the other children's fathers. Wheatley Street was right in the middle of the city centre in a location around Pool Meadow bus station and opposite what is now the Sports & Leisure Centre.

After a year or so Len bought a house in Cheveral Avenue, Radford and Pat left Wheatley Street and went to Radford Junior School. She liked it better there and she seemed have an easier time fitting in. Around 1939/40 when Pat was six or seven and at the outbreak of war the family decided to move out of Coventry and to Hilda's mother's house in Humphriss Street, Warwick. Margaret (Mags) Wilkins and her husband William (Bill) lived alone and across the road Hilda's older brother, also Bill, lived with his wife Maud and their children Don and David.

Coventry was a target for the German bombers because of the concentration of munition and armament factories and it was not considered safe for children. Len stayed on in Coventry to look after the house, to continue his work and as mentioned in a previous chapter, he joined the Home Guard and was an air raid warden during the Blitz and out most nights. He came out to Warwick to visit whenever he could.

Pat went to Emscote Road School in Warwick and enjoyed it, partly because her teacher was Uncle Frank, Len's younger brother, and she felt she was given slightly preferential treatment. Her other grandma Len's mother, Amy Rainbow, lived in Emscote Road and although Pat passed the house every day on her way to and from school, she rarely visited. She was a little afraid of Amy as she had lots of cats. Pat has never liked cats.

After their house was destroyed in Coventry during the blitz of 1941 Len was called up to join the RAF and Pat continued to live in Warwick with her grandmother and mother. During this time her Uncle Herbert, Len's youngest brother almost became a surrogate father to her. Pat had begun ballet lessons in Leamington Spa and every Saturday, after ballet, Herbert would take her to the Cadena Cafe in the Parade and treat her to cake. She said she felt like a princess and she became very close to Herbert and admits to feeling a teeny bit jealous when he first met his wife to be, Marjorie. Herbert worked at Lockheed in Leamington and his job was a reserved occupation, which is why he wasn't called up.

When the German attacks started in earnest it was not unusual for lone German pilots to fly in low over the town and strafe civilians. This happened to Pat on one occasion on her way home from school and was possibly the same time that another young girl in Warwick, at home in her bedroom, was wounded in the knee by a machine gun bullet when a German aircraft fired on the town. These were frightening times for children but something that most, including Pat, took in their stride.

Even though there was rationing it didn't affect Pat too much. Her grandmother had an orchard and grew all types of fruit and vegetables and her extended family lived on a farm in Lighthorne, Warwickshire – they kept pigs and were able to provide the family with meat. The rationing probably had more effect on the adults; Pat didn't seem to find it too bad. She said a lot of people complained about the lack of bananas, but she didn't like bananas anyway!

When Len came home from the war he bought another house in Sandy Lane, Coventry to rent out. Their own house wasn't fit to live in so they rented rooms off two elderly spinsters next door while it was being rebuilt. They wanted to stay close, as there was a problem with squatters moving into empty homes during this period. There were very many people who had been made homeless after the bombing.

Len's return home was a great relief for the family but Pat also said she was a bit wary of him, and didn't know quite how he was going to react. For many families this was a difficult period. When the men were away the women and children left behind made the best of it and developed their own lives. Readjusting to having husband and father home was not always easy after several years apart.

At this point in their lives Len and Hilda would have liked to have another baby but it wasn't to be. This was probably fortunate for Pat who was already feeling a little pushed out after Len's return.

The pastimes enjoyed by Pat were typical of the day; snakes and ladders and marbles, with her favourite toy being a pram. She used to walk for miles pushing her dolls and would sometimes walk from Warwick to Leamington Spa (about 3 miles) to meet her mum from work. She would occasionally go to the cinema with her cousin Don and would also go on outings with her best friend from school - Warwick Castle was a favourite destination, to chase the peacocks!

The family were not strongly religious although she did go to church every Sunday and remembers that she would take a short cut through her grandma's orchard. The services were High Church and Pat wasn't too impressed particularly as she hated the smell of incense. Her cousin, Don used to swing the incense and made sure he found where she was sitting so he could swing it as near to her as possible. She also went to Sunday school at the church and remembers that the only prize she ever received was for good attendance.

Pat can't recall ever having pocket money as such but says she was never kept short of money and if she needed something she would ask and it was usually given. She generally liked school - her favourite lessons were 'composition' and spelling. She hated arithmetic and sports, with the exception of netball. She was on the school team.

When she was eleven she took the 11+ examination and Len was keen that she passed so that she could go to the grammar school. On the day of the exam she came home and told her Dad that she thought she'd done well, at least with the section on how to abbreviate the names of English cities. Len asked her what her answer had been for short version of Birmingham and she replied, triumphantly, "Brum!" Len wasn't impressed and she didn't pass the exam. No grammar school for Pat but she loved her time at Barker Butts Secondary School.

She left school at 15 with dreams of working in a shop, but a chance remark by her cousin Joyce to her parents saw her getting a job at the car manufacturers, Armstrong Siddeley as a punch card operator. Pat has no idea what she was punching and why; the job was short lived and she moved into the office. Her next job was at the Danish Bacon factory, also in the office, as a typist and it was here that she met my Dad, Derek. The other girls warned her off him because he had a 'bad reputation' for dating lots of girls. A man from the wholesale branch of Danish Bacon, Neville asked her out on a date and when she agreed to meet him Derek was jealous and annoyed that she chose to date Neville and not him. When Pat met Neville in Broadgate (in the centre of Coventry) he was wearing a white, fringed silk scarf and she hoped they were going to the cinema so nobody she knew would see them! Eventually she relented and agreed to go out with Derek and the rest, as they say, is history.

She left Danish Bacon to work at Rugby Autocar on Queen Victoria Road where she was a typist and telephone operator. She suffered some health problems during this time and got the sack for taking too much time off sick.

When she was eighteen Derek did the right thing and asked Len for permission to marry his daughter, he agreed and they were engaged.

Pat's next job was at the Jaguar car plant working in the typing pool, up until their marriage in February 1954. After their marriage they moved in with Gran Rainbow. She had begun to require more attention in her old age, so her sons decided she should move to Coventry to be nearer her family. Her house in Emscote Road was sold, she moved to Grangemouth Drive and Pat and Derek moved in with her.

During early pregnancy with her first child (me!) Pat slipped down a kerb causing a threatened miscarriage. She had to give up work and have complete bed rest for two and a half months. It was felt that it was too much for her to continue living with Gran Rainbow and the doctor said she could be moved but only if they drove very slowly on the journey. It was at this point that Pat and Derek moved in with Len and Hilda at Cheveral Avenue and a few weeks later I was born.

Other Researchers

This brings us full circle and seems a fitting place to finish documenting this particular branch of the Rainbow family.

Although I have been involved with this research for a long time and, for the most part, it has been a solitary occupation, there are times when I've collaborated with and been helped by other researchers. The relationship has often been initiated via an email after noticing that a fellow historian is researching the same family branch at a genealogy site such as Genes Reunited.

I've had a lot of fun discovering new, albeit distant, cousins and two heads are certainly better than one at trying to unravel some of the more puzzling family mysteries.

Currently the UK genealogy website, Genes Reunited provides a service called Hot Matches, sending out an email to subscribers with links to other researchers working on the same family tree. More often than not these leads go nowhere - sending a link to another researcher who also has a Mary Smith, born 1902 rarely makes for a genuine connection. However, I usually scan the list to see if there is anyone that I haven't had contact with before and who is researching 'my' branch of the Rainbows. In 2003 I noticed that 'David' had James and Sarah Rainbow in his family tree and I dropped him a line to see if he would like to share information.

This was the start of a journey to prove that Dave and I were indeed fourth cousins. Dave told me that his great grandfather Percy Joyce married a Sarah Emily Rainbow in 1902 in Eastbourne. The only Sarah Rainbow that he could find that matched in age was Sarah Rainbow, the daughter of Joseph John Rainbow (son of James and Sarah). All well and good but 'my' Sarah was Coventry born and on the surface, I couldn't find any link with the south coast.

Dave had established that Percy Joyce had moved with his family to Bromley in Bow in London from Surrey somewhere between 1891 and 1901 and he had become a furniture dealer's clerk. On the 1891 census Percy was living in a lodging house in Tottenham Court Road, off Euston Road in London with many other furniture dealer workers.

I'd lost 'my' Sarah E. and her family after the 1881 census, they seemed to have disappeared. At first I thought there was a possibility they had emigrated which would then mean, of course, that she wasn't the Sarah that married Percy. However some further searching and I found them on the 1891 census. The whole family had moved to London and were living in two rooms in Kenton Road, Bloomsbury, off Euston Road, a little further up from Percy with only University College London between them. She worked as an upholsterer's assistant.

So we surmised between us that Sarah Emily and Percy, both in the furniture trade and living only streets away from each other might have met at work. It certainly looked much more plausible that this was the correct Sarah Rainbow. In the 1901 census I again had trouble tracking down Sarah, but found her living with a friend in rooms at 77, St. Augustine's Road, St. Pancreas using her middle name, Emily.

Apart from the obvious advantages of new technology, ie the digitising of records, there are other revelations brought about by not such obvious developments. Google Street View enables us to look at current photographs of streets and houses and if we are lucky the houses that our ancestors lived in are still standing and we can 'walk' along their road and see what they saw. St. Augustine's Road still exists and I imagine that the large Victorian houses do not look so very different, at least on the outside, as they did in Sarah E. Rainbow's day.

The next step was to order Percy and Sarah's wedding certificate. If it confirmed that Sarah was born in Coventry and her father's name was Joseph then we had an almost definite match. Dave sent off for the certificate and we waited with bated breath. A few days later and an email arrived from Dave. The unequivocal headline was "WE ARE COUSINS!!". We had a match.

Further confirmation came recently when the 1911 census revealed that Percy and Sarah were alive and well and living at 86, Southfield Road, Bedford Park, London. Percy was a jeweller's assistant and Sarah had again reverted to using her middle name Emily.

The only reason we can think of that they married in Eastbourne is that Percy was born in Sussex so maybe there was a family connection there.

Another collaboration of research happened when I was trying to track down the elusive Lillie Blanche Rainbow, actress and daughter of Joseph (J.G) Rainbow and Emma (nee Sharman). Sue, who is related to Emma, contacted me and we swapped many emails with our theories regarding the enigma that was Lillie Blanche such as; What happened to Lillie? Why was Emma referred to as J.G's daughter in a publication about the theatre and were Lillie and Emma actually the same person using different names? Sue spent long hours researching in the stage newspapers (before they were digitised) and piecing together the clues. Sadly, I lost touch with her and have no idea if she made the same exciting discoveries that I have about the acting branch of the Rainbow family.

Mary in Australia is related to Kitty Curzons, the second wife of Joseph Rainbow (son of John Rainbow and Ruth, nee Hurst). Mary and I exchanged many emails about our connection and it was only with her help that I discovered that Joseph was not born in Coventry as I had assumed. I was able to break through my 'brick wall' and discovered the early Rainbows originated from Cotesabach in Leicestershire.

Linda is my second cousin, daughter of the late Herbert and Marjorie Rainbow. We got together via the Internet and she was able to share some valuable information and photos particularly about her grandfather, and my great grandfather Percy. She had photos that I had never seen and memorabilia such as exam certificates and a memorial card, which were wonderful.

More recently, as mentioned earlier, I've made a connection with Cotesabach, the earliest home of the Rainbows, in the person of Sophy Newton, the Manager of Cotesabach Estate. The Marriotts and Rainbows appear to have had links for at least a century and a half, from 1764 when

Robert Marriott was the owner of the Cotesbach estate and William Rainbow was Overseer of the Poor for the village, right through to at least 1905. Although the Rainbows had moved to Lutterworth by that time, the Cotesbach receipts reveal their services or goods were still being purchased by the Marriotts. It's been very exciting to renew that relationship in the twenty first century. I have hopes that the archives at Cotesbach Hall may yet reveal more about William Rainbow of Shawell and his origins.

I'm sure there are many others that have shared snippets of information and have helped move my research forward either via emails or online forums and messages boards. If you were one of them, thank you!

The motivation for documenting my research shifted slightly during the writing process and I found that I became more focused on teasing out some of the incredible stories that lay hidden just under the surface of the basic genealogical data. There is always a slight nagging feeling that I have overlooked some important, but yet to be discovered story. I'll have to save that for volume two!

Written June 2010 - March 2011

Appendix

Obituary of Joseph George Rainbow
1839 - 1893
Published in The Era, September 1893

The late Mr J. G. Rainbow

To the Editor of the Era

Sir, As a tribute of respect, one may be permitted to say a word as to the actor-manager whose sudden death caused such a shock to his friends, and they were legion. It is not given to many men, either in or out of the profession to be so popular and to be so genuinely liked as was the late Mr J.G. Rainbow, or as his intimates called him, and as he liked to be called, "Joe Rainbow". Being one of the old school of actors whom few - very few - are now left, and being both a resident and travelling manager, his name was a household word in the profession; but amongst the vast number of his friends and acquaintances there would not be found one who could justly say a word against him. He was so innately kind-hearted and had such a fund of good humour that everyone of necessity, liked him, and everyone who had business relations with him found that his word was as good as his bond.

Mr Rainbow raised the West Bromwich theatre to a position it never attained before; indeed, he had such indomitable energy that he could 'rush' almost anything into a success. He worked hard for what he obtained. Throughout his long theatrical career he had seen every phase of the profession: he had gone thoroughly through the mill - as everyone should, though no one does in these degenerate times. He learnt the rudiments of his art in a Birmingham amateur theatrical club, of which - to give only two instances - Messers Carter-Edwards and Edward Price were, at the time, members. Mr Rainbow's first engagement, or almost first, was at the Theatre Royal, Hanley, from thence he went to Theatre Royal, Birmingham under Messers Simpsons and afterwards graduated in stock companies, going through the usual curriculum, until he blossomed into a manager. One of his early theatrical enterprises was a ten-week stock season at Theatre Royal,

Shrewsbury. Shrewsbury is a picturesque town on a fine river; but theatrically speaking it does not strike one as a potential gold mine.

Mr Rainbow, however, by sheer hard work on and off stage made the stock season pay. He had a good all-round company, Miss Emma Rainbow of course being the chief attraction, and the season was a very pleasant one to all concerned. Bridlington Quay was his next venture, and soon after he started Mortimer Murdoch's piece *Proved True*. This he toured till 1885 when he started *Main Hope*, the work of an obscure member of his former Shrewsbury company.

In 1887 he started *Lucky Star*, the work of the same obscure member, and in the spring of this year he produced *Wheel of Time*. Mr Rainbow's chief work, however, lay at West Bromwich. The theatre itself is wonderfully improved specially behind the scenes. He had most of the best travelling companies and business was very different to what it used to be.

In the town he was personally well known and esteemed. He was continually urged to be a Town Councillor, but his heart and soul were in his profession, and to that only he cared to confine his attention. Many a one will miss his kindly greeting at the theatre. His quips and cranks and amusing anecdotes made him 'good company'. Dullness would not reign where he was: and even throughout this year, when he was tortured by a wretched cough, he ever sustained his genial good spirits.

King Death is rapidly thinning the ranks of the old school of actors; the loss of any one of them is a matter for regret; for it weakens a profession that is now jumped into rather than learnt: but when the loss is attended with the circumstances such as those which attended the death of Mr Rainbow it not only is grievious it is appalling, since the ruthless hand of the Great Unseen fell so unexpectedly, and did its dread work so quickly. There are two persons in particular to whom this loss will be irreparable: may those two persons understand that they have the condolences and heartfelt sympathy of all who were considered friends of poor Joe Rainbow. Your obedient servant, REMOC. September 11th 1893.

Obituary Henry Rainbow 1833 - 1913

Coventry Herald, February 1913

By the death of Mr. H. Rainbow, which took place at his residence in Lincoln Street on Monday last, Coventry has lost a well-known citizen. In his 80th year he had been in failing health for some months.

Mr Rainbow came from an old weaving family but he was in business for many years in Market Street as a restaurant keeper retiring after a successful career several years ago. In his long life he was connected with with many local interests. For instance he was for a time a member of the Board of Guardians and for a quarter of a century a trustee of the Church General Burial Society. He was on the committee of the Provident Dispensary, was connected with the Industrial Land and Provident Building Society and was one of the Seniority Fund (Freemen's) Trustees. In politics he was a Liberal and was a member of the Liberal Association.

Mr Rainbow gave the best of his services to the church in Well Street, with which he was associated for 44 years being a deacon for 36 years and senior deacon for 16 years. He was also treasurer of many of the church funds. Another office he held was that of treasurer of the Warwickshire Congregational Union.

The funeral took place at the Cemetery yesterday. A service was held at the Well Street chapel, the Pastor (Rev. Thomas Goodman) conducting it. The following hymns were sung "Oh God, Our Help In Ages Past", "Light After Darkness" and "Now The Labourer's Task Is O'er". In the course of a brief address Rev. T. Goodman said,

Henry Rainbow, our beloved friend and brother, after serving his own generation by the will of God, has fallen on sleep.

We bring into the House of prayer all that is left of him here, - the poor fallen tenement - and gather together in reverence and thoughtfulness for these last tender offices of faith and love.

Here, where he worshipped God, where he often saw the vision of Christ, where he bore his witness to the reality of things spiritual and Divine, where he stood with unwavering fidelity for so many years as a standard bearer for the Christ to whom he was pledged, and for the church he loved so well.

Very few men have so long, so continuously, so patiently and so willingly fulfilled the sacred trust of service in the Christian Church as our departed friend.

Led here more than half a century ago, he has filled in the whole of that long period with earnest work, responding to every call, answering every demand, never being out of office until a few months ago he had reluctantly through physical weakness, to lay down one thing after another of the work he so much loved.

For 44 years his name has been on the roll of the Church; at the time of his deceased only two names stood in precedence before him on the sacred register.

A deacon of the church for 36 years and the senior deacon for 16 years and no one ever disputed his right or his fitness to be a deacon of the Church. He won his place and held his office by sterling merit, by consistency of life, by plenitude of service. During many years he held the position of treasurer to the Church's funds and did a praiseworthy part. As financial officer he was scrupulously careful. I never knew a more trustworthy man. It was deeply touching to hear him in his last illness as we talked together, "Is everything quite straight and right?" And when assured, he would add. "Yes, I have tried to keep all things clear and correct."

He had an interest in many things in the city, where he was well known. A Trustee of the Church General Burial Society for upwards of a quarter of a century, a member of the Board of Guardians for some years, on the committees of the Provident Dispensary, the Industrial and Provident Land and Building Society, the Friendly and Provident Institution, he did good service.

But as he gave his best to the church of his choice, and here his sterling qualities were best known. Those qualities were not of a showy kind but of a solid quiet character. He was without ostentation, a grave, practical, matter of fact man, to whom duty was sacred and its fulfilment his satisfaction. Much of the puritan was in his composition and in the habit of his life. There was strength in him - strength of purpose, strength of conviction. Loyalty to truth marked him, firmness of grip and a calm endurance.

No winds of passion, nor tremors of excitement were seen in him. Equable patient self possessed he held on his way. He was the very personification of uprightness, integrity and common sense. Perhaps a little of the emotional and fervent would have given a richer tone to his life. But we were proud of him, and gave him the esteem and confidence of our souls. Our departed friend was one of the worthiest of men - one of the best Christ ever gave to His Church. A lover of the old Evangelical faith, devoted to the church, kind and helpful to others in manifold ways, sturdy as a Free Churchman. Keeping without any desire for praise, steadily at his work, always at his post, always bearing his witness, and while enthusiasts come and go, he stood "four square to every wind that blew" Fulfilling Micah's word: Do justly, love mercy, and walk humbly with thy God."

We realise a great loss in the passing of our dear brother, but we thank God for him and bring our tribute to his memory in the House of God and fore fancy the day when our hopes shall be consummated and we shall find our fellow labourers and our loved ones in the ampler life to which our departed friend has gone. Certainly for him the word has been spoken, "Well done, good and faithful servant," etc.

For dear ones of his home, we breathe our tender words of love and prayer.

There was a large attendance at the graveside. The bearers were Messers J Richardson, W. Matthews, E. Matthews, T. Stringer, R. Wright and E. Farmer. The mourners were Mrs Rainbow (widow), Miss A Rainbow (daughter), Mrs Parnell (sister), Mr Edwin Rainbow (brother), Mr P Rainbow (nephew) Mr H Rainbow (nephew), Mr H Briscoe (Warwick), Mr and Mrs G. Coulson (brother in law and sister) and the deacons of the church, Messers J. T. Moy, H. T. Garlick, H. Wakelin, W. T. Hows, J. G. Morgan and E. Marson. Wreaths were sent from the officers of the Church Burial Society, pastor and deacons of Well Street Church, Well Street Young Women's Society, Well Street Young Women's Bible Class, Well Street C.E. Society, Rev T. And Mrs Goodman and family. Executors of George Storer, Mr and Mrs W Bird and family, Mr and Mrs E Marson, Mr and Mrs M. Stokes, Mr and Mrs E. A. Stokes, Mr and Mrs Sleath (Llangollen) Mr and Mrs Philpin and family. Mr and Mrs H.T. Atkins, Mr and Mrs C. Anthony, Mr and Mrs A Curtis, Mr and Mrs Yardly, Mr and Mrs Wilson, Mr and Mrs Dauncey, A. Newton, Emma and Fan, George, Arthur, Bert and Sidney, George and Edie, Pollie and Jennie and 'Evington', Queen Victoria Road.

At Well Street Congregational Church on Sunday night a special 'In Memoriam' service will be conducted by the Pastor, the Rev. Thomas Goodman. Appropriate music will be rendered by the choir.

Obituaries of Edwin Rainbow

Coventry Herald 11/1/1918 11/12th January 1918, Coventry Herald

DEATH OF MR. EDWIN RAINBOW

We regret to announce the death of Mr. Edwin Rainbow, which occurred at his residence, 30, Queen's Road, Coventry, on Wednesday evening. The deceased gentleman, who was 66 years of age, was a widower, his wife having died in 1909. He leaves three sons. Mr Rainbow had been in his usual state of health until Tuesday evening last and rose as usual next morning, when he complained of having had a restless night. About eight o'clock on Wednesday morning he became seriously ill, and lapsed into unconsciousness. Dr. Ballantyne, who lives near, was immediately sent for, and at once attended. Mr Rainbow, however, never regained consciousness and passed away shortly after six o'clock in the evening.

Mr Rainbow was a journalist by profession, and for many years occupied a responsible position upon the " Coventry Herald and Free Press" as it was then known. Eventually he became Secretary of the Coventry Technical Institute, and later he also held the secretaryship of the Coventry School of Art. Upon the administration of the Elementary Education Act., 1902, these posts were abolished. Deceased took a prominent part in the organising of the Science Lectures For The People, which were given in the city some years ago. He was interested in Coventry Shorthand Writers Association, of which he was for some time president.

Mr Rainbow held for many years past the office of Registrar of Births and Deaths for Coventry southwest, and previously for the sub-district of St. John. In each of these appointments he showed ability and precision and fulfilled the duties throughout in a most efficient manner Mr Rainbow especially interested himself in the work of adult schools. For a number of years he was a teacher at Lords Street Early Morning School and latterly had officiated as teacher of a Young Men's Class at Queen's Road Baptist Church at which place of worship he was a regular attendant.

Obituary Standard 11/1/1918 11th/12th January 1918, Coventry Standard

Death of Mr E. Rainbow A Useful Career

We regret to announce the death of Mr. Edwin Rainbow, which occurred at his residence 30, Queens Road, Coventry on Wednesday evening. Mr Rainbow was 66 years of age and a widower, his wife having died in 1909. He leaves 3 sons. He was in his usual state of health up to Tuesday evening last but on Wednesday morning, on rising, he complained of having had a restless night. About 8 o'clock in the morning he became seriously ill and lapsed into unconsciousness. Dr Ballantyne, who resides near, was at once sent for, and promptly attended. Mr Rainbow, however, never regained consciousness and passed away shortly after 6 o'clock in the evening.

Mr Rainbow began life as a printer and served his apprenticeship in the office of The Coventry Standard. At the termination of his "seven years" he found an engagement in the office of The Coventry Times where he also became a printers reader. In the meantime he had learnt to write shorthand and after a few years at the "Times" he removed to The Coventry Herald office where he was engaged as a general literary assistant to the late Mr. J.M. Scott.

While at the Herald office he did work for a number of newspapers and he became widely known as any journalist in the district. He was a very capable man and in the early days of Mr Scott's proprietorship of the "Herald" he was left in charge for long periods while Mr Scott resided in London. In consequence of conditions, which arose in

1895, he gave up local journalism, although he retained much of his outside connections and a little later he was appointed by the Board of Guardians to the office of Registrar of Births and Deaths for the sub-district of St. John's rendered vacant by the death of Mr. John Blundell. He retained office in the recent revision of the local sub-districts and continued to hold it to the end.

Mr Rainbow gave considerable assistance to the late Aid. Timmons, the later Mr John Rotherham ... (rest of this line was indecipherable!) Technical Institute on a voluntary basis and after a time he became secretary of the Coventry School of Art and held both offices until the passing of the Elementary School Act of 1902 when the administration of the school was changed. In each of the posts he showed ability and precision and fulfilled the duties throughout in a most efficient manner.

He was a Baptist by religious conviction and for very many years was a member of the St. Michael's Baptist Community. He was always ready to give any movement his assistance and was especially interested in the work of adult schools. For a number of years he was a teacher in Lord Street Early Morning School and latterly he was officiated as teacher of a young men's class at Queen's Road Baptist Church of which place of worship he was a regular attendant. He was well known in political circles as an ardent Liberal. He was an excellent speaker and was held in the highest esteem by a large circle of friends who will deeply regret his demise.

Obituary response - Coventry Standard

Jan 18th/19th 1918

I do not think the writers of the memoirs did full justice to Mr Rainbow's work as a compiler and an author. It was quite the custom at one time, if a public record were required, to entrust the compilation to him. He produced the official record of Queen Victoria's Jubilee in 1887 and her Diamond Jubilee in 1897. He wrote 'Walks Through Coventry' the interesting guidebook published by Messrs Caldicott and Feltham:

he is generally credited with preparation of the recently issued history of the Coventry Co-operative Society.

He was on two or three occasions an accredited member of journalistic deputations to Bohemia and other states in the Near East and he wrote in the Coventry Standard very interesting impressions of his journeys and investigations. He was an industrious writer for various publications and was generally busy on some literary work when his official duties as Registrar of Births and Deaths gave him time.

Some years ago Mr Rainbow frequently contributed to this letter especially in 1907 when a Godiva procession was held for the hospital in consequence of ***** herein, he wrote interestingly on the character the pageant should assume and there is reason to believe that his comments were not without effect. He wrote many leaders in the Coventry Herald and was undoubtedly one of the best-known journalists of his day. Of late years he was more privately engaged and in consequence of this and of the changing population he was less well known. But the files of the newspapers contain a standing record of his work in the chronicling of the history of the city in former times.

This is a selection of extracts from newspapers that mention Edwin Rainbow and are an illustration of his involvement in the community along with his interest in further education particularly science and his desire to see the evolution of trades in Coventry recognised by a museum.

Coventry Herald, Ist February 1895

"SOME ASPECTS OF EDUCATION"

On Tuesday evening, at the Coventry Liberal Club, Mr. Edwin Rainbow lectured on the above subject, Mr. J. Morton presiding. After describing the system of commercial education obtaining in Holland , the lecturer suggested various points in which the system of commercial education in this country might be improved, especially in regard to the study of geography, arithmetic, and modern languages. He also advocated the formation in Coventry of a museum, one of the features of which should be the illustration of the evolution of local trades. Mr J. Thomas, in proposing a vote of thanks to Mr. Rainbow, expressed the hope that some practical result may follow the delivery of this lecture. Mr H. Tomson seconded the vote, which was carried with acclamation. A vote of thanks to the chairman concluded the proceedings.

Coventry Herald, 1st February 1895

"SUBSCRIPTION READING ROOM"

On Friday night the annual meeting of the members was held at the Technical Institute. Mr T. B. R. Ball presided and the report and statements of accounts were passed. The retiring committee Messers W. A. Pizzie, T. Robinson, E. Rainbow, T.B.R. Ball, T. I. Johnson,

T. Checkland and W. Kirk (hon. sec), were re-elected. Mr Kirk was thanked for his services as hon. sec during the past year.

Coventry Herald, 1895

COVENTRY TECHNICAL INSTITUTE

The secretary of the Coventry Technical Institute (Mr E. Rainbow) has received the results of a number of the Society of Arts examinations, 1895 as follows: Bookkeeping First Class: Charles F. Cramp. Second Class: Arthur Tallow. Third Class: Isabel A. Gray, Mary E. Perkins, Elizabeth Smith, Ada Wheatley. Domestic Economy, First Class and Bronze Medal: Sarah Burbidge. First Class: May Castle, Minnie L.M. Frith, Edith Hancox. 2nd Class: Lizzie Brooks, Nellie Collett, Mary A. P. Cure, Catherine Liggins, Sarah J. Lowe, Alice M. M. Reeve, Jessie E. Seymour, Helen Walker. French: 2nd Class: Charles Dolphin. 3rd Class: Thomas L. Husserby. German 3rd Class: Reginald H. Lord, Alice M. Loveitt. Alathea W. N. Seymour. Music, Rudiments: Higher Grade: Nellie Amos, Thomas G. Dauncy, Bertha Grant, Jessie Green, Rose E. Green, Hilda A. S. Jones, Emily M. Lister, Sarah A. Palmer, Caroline C. Tidy, Kate Topp, Arthur W. Wincott. Elementary Grade: Edwin Brooknell, Ethel M Pearson, Clara Welton. Music, Harmony: Elementary Grade. Henry Shaw, Jessie Green, Eleanor Mary Pick, Kate Topp. Shorthand: 2nd Class: Richard A Foley, Alice E. Lester. 3rd Class: Herbert Lord, Amy A. W. Rainbow, (Edwin's niece) Thomas Timerick, William Tomlinson. Typewriting: 2nd Class: Herbert W. Grimsley. The names are not in order of merit.

Chasing Rainbows

WITH LOVE FROM DADDY - LETTERS FROM THE WAR

Letters from Leonard Rainbow to his daughter, Patricia, then aged 11, written during in 1945. These are unedited and are included, with the caveat that they contain occasional and unfortunate racist references.

>1037534 LAC Rainbow
>
>H West
>
>40 Staging Post
>
>Royal Air Force
>
>Iraq & Persia
>
>29th March 1945
>
>Dear Pat

It was lovely to have your two nice long letters waiting for me when I arrived here. I expect Mummy has had her letter and you will know where I am. You would have liked to have been with me through Palestine to see the orange groves and palm trees. It is a nice country. It wasn't far from where Jesus was born, at one time of my journey we passed very near Nazareth. I should like to have spent a few days there and visited some of the places of the Bible stories.

When you see the country and people with their quaint dresses you can understand those stories a lot better. Some of the men wear white head dress flowing down their back with black bands round the top of the head, others wear red and white, others black and some wear a kind of red top hat without the brim and nearly all of them wear long flowing robes, mostly white, but some have different colours, it depends on what religion they are.

The native women hide themselves a lot and when they do go out they hide their faces with a veil.

Where I am now we have nice billets and the "Chicko" (a native boy) polishes our boots, makes our bed and does the washing. He comes round first thing in the morning when we are asleep and collects our boots so when we wake up they are nice and clean. What do you think of that? I should like to explain lots to you, but cannot do it all at once. Looking out of my window I see the tennis courts and in the distance the NAAFI, where we can still get cups of tea with a little more sugar in than in England. Nearly all the buildings have big electric fans hanging from the ceilings but its not warm enough yet for them.

I was very pleased to hear that you are looking after Mummy so well, so I shall be thinking of you Saturday mornings having your coffee at the Porridge Pot and wishing I was with you. It was nice to hear you had been out into the country, it must be nice with some of the early Spring flowers out.

It is not too hot here yet, just nice and warm with a breeze blowing. I went to the Cinema this evening, first house so I left your letter for a little while. It wasn't a very good film, Bette Davis in "Old Acquaintance" but it is a very nice cinema, about the size of the Regal in Leamington Spa. They are hard, tip-up seats but not too bad for a couple of hours. It was a free show tonight and they change the film every night and have 2 or 3 free shows during the week so I am not too badly off, am I? It's really a very nice camp and far better than any I have heard of in England. There is a also a big swimming pool which is opening next week! I think!! So I shall be able to have a swim and keep cool.

Now Pat it is nearly bed time, I expect you are getting ready as well because it is 8pm by your time and 10pm here, so we must go to bed about the same time, don't we? I shall be anxious to know how you got on and I know you have done your best how ever you got on.

So night night dear. Sleep tight.

Lots of love and kisses

From Your Daddy

Xxxxx

1037534 LAC Rainbow

H West

40 Staging Post

Royal Air Force

Iraq & Persia

18th April 1945

Dear Pat

I was very pleased to get your letter and to hear you were enjoying your holiday. You sound as if you have had a real good time. How were the ices? Were they as good as we had at Blackpool? I haven't seen any out here at all I expect they would have a job to keep the ice!!

Well Pat, I haven't much to tell you this time, I haven't been out of the camp since I arrived but am hoping to get a 48 hour on Monday 16th April to go into Baghdad. You have probably heard about that place so look it up on your map. Have you been following where I have been right from Egypt through Palestine to Hiafa. You will see how near I was to Jerusalem and Nazareth. I have heard we are not very far from the Garden of Eden but how true that is I can't tell you as there are a number of places which claim that, like in England there are 2 or 3 place that claim to be the centre.

I shall probably have more to tell you when I have been to Baghdad and seen the shops and historical places.

I am very pleased you are looking after Mummy so well for me. Keep it up and take her out and enjoy yourselves. It won't be for much longer, then I shall be able to take you out. What a time we shall have!!

You would like the weather here now. It is lovely and warm without being too hot, you would be able to wear all your summer dresses without fear of getting cold, it gets dark about 7.30pm but there are plenty of lights about, there is no blackout. Won't it be nice when all the shops are lit up again at home - really bright.

Now Pat, as its nearly bedtime I must write to Mummy as well so I shall have to say Night Night!

Don't forget to look after Mummy for me, will you? And look after yourself too. It won't be very long now before I shall be seeing you again.

Cheerio Pat

Love and kisses

From Daddy

xxxxx

(pat in kisses)

1037534 LAC Rainbow

H West

40 Staging Post

Royal Air Force

Iraq & Persia

18th April 1945

Dear Pat

I was very pleased to get your letter and to hear you were enjoying your holiday. You sound as if you have had a real good time. How were the ices? Were they as good as we had at Blackpool? I haven't seen any out here at all I expect they would have a job to keep the ice!!

Well Pat, I haven't much to tell you this time, I haven't been out of the camp since I arrived but am hoping to get a 48 hour on Monday 16th April to go into Baghdad. You have probably heard about that place so look it up on your map. Have you been following where I have been right from Egypt through Palestine to Hiafa. You will see how near I was to Jerusalem and Nazareth. I have heard we are not very far from the Garden of Eden but how true that is I can't tell you as there are a number of places which claim that, like in England there are 2 or 3 place that claim to be the centre.

I shall probably have more to tell you when I have been to Baghdad and seen the shops and historical places.

I am very pleased you are looking after Mummy so well for me. Keep it up and take her out and enjoy yourselves. It won't be for much longer, then I shall be able to take you out. What a time we shall have!!

You would like the weather here now. It is lovely and warm without being too hot, you would be able to wear all your summer dresses without fear of getting cold, it gets dark about 7.30pm but there are plenty of lights about, there is no blackout. Won't it be nice when all the shops are lit up again at home - really bright.

Now Pat, as its nearly bedtime I must write to Mummy as well so I shall have to say Night Night!

Don't forget to look after Mummy for me, will you? And look after yourself too. It won't be very long now before I shall be seeing you again.

Cheerio Pat

Love and kisses

From Daddy

xxxxx

(pat in kisses)

1037534 LAC Rainbow

H West

40 Staging Post

Royal Air Force

Iraq & Persia

22nd May 1945

Dear Pat

I was very pleased to get your letter, it was a lovely long one, you are getting better every time.

I notice your date stamp is still working. It looks quite smart on the top of your letters.

You sound as if you had a nice time on VE day, it was quite strange and new to you to see all the flood lighting, wasn't it?

I should like to have been with you, but we shall have a good time together when I come home for good.

I didn't hear the wireless you mentioned, we do not hear it very often. They have got a small set in the NAAFI in a little room at the back but it isn't very clear and unless there is something very special on we don't bother to go over.

I am afraid there isn't much news I can tell you from here. It is very hot but not too unbearable, it would be nice if we had an English summer like it for a change, wouldn't it?

Did you see the snaps I sent in Mummy's letter. Did you notice how the Chicko's plonked themselves right in the front? Did you like the one of the inside of the Church. It hardly seems possible to have such a nice place right in the middle of a desert, does it?

I shall try to get some more for you when I get the chance. I don't think I ever told you about the money here did I?

There is a Dinar that is the Iraq pound. Then you get 1/2 Dinar and 1/4 Dinar (10/= & 5/=). All the coins are counted up in Fils, the largest I have come across is the 50 fil piece equal to our own 1/= and about the same size. I Fil is about one farthing, the same size as our farthing too. Can you follow that so far. The next is a 2 Fil piece (or halfpenny) 10 files (2 1/2) 4 Fils (1d) and is about all the coins.

As you will see they use paper money quite a lot as there is a 5/= note. So if you change a Dinar you get 15/= in notes. I wonder if you can follow it! Don't forget to let me know! I thought you might be interested!

Now, Pat, I must get on with Mummy's letter. I think your Victory greeting at the end of your letter was perfect. I won't try even if I could think of a one better because it is exactly what I wish.

So night, night Pat.

Love and kisses

from

Daddy

(pat spelled out in kisses)

1037534 LAC Rainbow

H West

40 Staging Post

Royal Air Force

Iraq & Persia

9th June 1945

Dear Pat

I was delighted to get your letter yesterday and to hear you are having such a nice holiday, but the weather isn't being very kind to you, is it? But perhaps it is waiting until your next holiday in August.

I don't think there is much to tell you Pat, all our spare time is spent on the bed in the billet except for going across to the NAAFI for lemonade. Very lazy, aren't we? But it gets very hot and that is the coolest spot with the electric fans going. I did go into Baghdad again the other week, I expect mummy told you. Have you found it on your map yet? I should like to have taken you round to see all the funny people. Some of them talk broken English. They are mostly the shopkeepers who want to sell you something. We went round the bazaars this time and what a place it was. I don't think I could describe it properly to you.

They were formed of lots of narrow passages all roofed over with stalls each side where they sold all kinds of junk. Chai (tea) is served black in a small tumbler very much like we have for wine. It is placed on a small saucer and there you have your cup of tea in Iraq. It is poured out of a big silver teapot, a long shaped affair very much like a big coffee pot. I haven't tasted any of it because it isn't wise to touch any food or drink outside a service club.

The men on the stalls wear all kinds of funny dresses. Some wear long white robes down to their feet just like a long nightdress, just as simple, no belt and long black beads with no headdress. They are the Christians, so they told us. The head dresses of the different Arab tribes and religions are too numerous to mention but if I tell you it looks more like a fancy dress parade you can guess the rest. We saw some of the temples, they are for worship (only from a distance) and there are some beautiful buildings.

I have got some snaps to show you when I come home, I won't rush sending any more. The most beautiful has 6 domes made of pure gold which glistens in the sun.

The children all run about bare footed with very little clothing on at all. Of course there are a few of the educated type who go to schools but you have to be very rich to afford that. The average child never goes to school and has to earn a living very early in life either by carrying goods, shoe blacking or begging! Not a very nice life, is it? So you see quite a number huddled up on the river banks at night, sleeping - the end of another day for them.

I think I have told you about the women, when I was there last you see very few about and never serving on the stalls, etc. They are completely covered from head to foot in black. I think after all I will rush sending you a snap of these because I can't describe them to you. As you will see they do all the hard work and carry nearly everything on their heads. A 5 gallon drum of water is nothing for them to cart about from place to place.

Well Pat, I think that will be all this time. I am glad to hear you are still looking after Mummy for me, it won't be long now before I shall be back and we can all have a good time together.

So Cheerio Pat

Love and kiss

from Daddy (Pat in kisses)

1037534 LAC Rainbow

H West

40 Staging Post

Royal Air Force

Iraq & Persia

13th August 1945

Dear Pat,

I was pleased to get your letter and to hear you had such a nice holiday, its a pity this beastly old war didn't finish a month or two earlier and then I should have been home to go with you. It will be a bit now for a seaside holiday, won't it?

Anyway Pat I should be home for your birthday, it will be nice if I can manage it won't it? It's on a Tuesday this year, so if I am home I will let you take me out. How's that? With Mummy of course. You can take us both out, unless you have got other plans!

It won't be long now before I start on that 3,600 mile journey back. It sounds a long way, doesn't it but it shouldn't take all that long. So look after Mummy for a little longer for me and then I shall be back to look after you both.

I expect you will soon be celebrating the end of the war with Japan, then it will all be over.

I am afraid I haven't much news for you. I haven't been out of the camp since I went to Baghdad in May. It's been too hot to do anything but keep in the cool. Can you imagine the temperature going up to 120 degrees and over that for 3 days recently. Oh!!! wasn't it hot! Even the ??? of the bed was hot, the only place it was cool was under the shower and then get right under the big fans. But it had dropped now to 112 - 115 degrees.

Well Pat, I am off to sleep now so Cheerio for now. It won't be long before I am back with you.

Love and kisses

from Daddy

(pat spelt out in kisses

7th October 1945

Dear Pat

I expect Mummy has been telling you where I am and how I am proceeding on my journey back home. I am afraid it is very slow just now and am getting very impatient to be on the move again. It is a fortnight last Thursday since we arrived in Egypt and first of all had two days in Cairo. I would rather have spent 16 days down there than here, there were some very interesting places to go and see. I only had time to have a very rushed visit to the Pyramids. The largest one in the world is here and I went inside it. Oh! What an adventure! We went in a small opening in the side and started climbing along dark narrow passages on our hands and knees part of the time. It was pitch dark all the way.

Halfway up was the King's Burial Chamber, only quite a small room where the Kings of thousands of years ago were embalmed and left. Of course the place is quite empty now all that was discovered is in Museums now. All of the carvings are done out of solid stone, the Queen's chamber is only a quarter of the way up. All in complete darkness, no openings or windows. We had one or two candles and the guide lit some magnesium tape for us to see the carvings in the chambers. There were 3 pyramids but we only saw the other two from a distance, then we saw the Sphinx. That is a huge thing carved out of a solid piece of rock. It has the head of a man, the face of a woman and the body of a lion. The guide told us that it was to represent the beauty of a woman, the brains of a man and the strength of a lion. I dare say we might think differently these days as to the outstanding qualities but that is what they thought in those days, about four thousand years ago and more.

Well Pat I am afraid I can't tell you very well in a letter all about the sights I saw but I hope very soon now to be home and then I can tell you. I thought I should be well on my way now and should not have to write to you.

It is very quiet here and we are just waiting patiently every day hoping for news of a boat. The sun is still shining every day and there is tons of sand as soon as we step out of our tents in the morning we are up to our ankles in it.

I expect you can find on the map just about where I am. About halfway down the Suez Canal there is a big lake (Bitter Lake). We can see that from our camp and the ships from India pass along there.

I suggested the other day going down there and trying to get a hitch home.

Well Pat I shall be home soon and we shall have lots to talk about and lots to do.

So Cheerio and look after Mummy just a little longer for me.

Night night dear

Love and kisses

from

Daddy

xxxxx

1037534 LAC Rainbow

H West

40 Staging Post

Royal Air Force

Iraq & Persia

28th August 1945

Dear Pat

I was pleased to get your nice long letter and to hear you had such a good time on V.J. night.

It was almost like the 5th November wasn't it, with all the bonfires and fireworks?

I expect your biggest excitement was going to London!!

What did you think of it all? You had read about the House of Parliament, Westminster Bridge, The Abbey and all the rest of the big places in London, but to actually see them is very different, isn't it?

Did you see the Guards in Whitehall? I hope you enjoyed your visit to the Zoo, there will be lots to see there.

I wonder if Mummy took you to Madame Tussauds, I don't think she will forget to go there because we went there the first time we visited London, a long time ago now and then we saw the first Talkie film in Tussaud's Cinema.

Well Pat you sound as if you enjoyed yourself by the letter I had, it will be all over when you get this letter but you will have a lot of things to remember from your first visit to London. You have been a very lucky girl this year with all the lovely holidays. I think you have got a lot of things to thank Mummy for, don't you?

Chasing Rainbows

I know you are doing all you can to help her, which shows more than anything else how much you appreciate all the lovely times she has given you. Now Pat, it is time for me to pack up, I have got to write to Mummy yet and it's nearly 10pm. So night night dear. I'll soon be home to see you again.

Love and kiss

from Daddy

(lots of kisses)

Bibliography

19th Century British Library Newspapers [Accessed June 8, 2010]

A Treatise On The Law Relating To Highways 1829, Robert Wellbeloved

A historical account of the services of the 34th Regiment of the Foot ... Available at: http://www.archive.org/stream/ahistoricalacco02noakgoog#page/n84/mode/1up [Accessed June 7, 2010].

Acland-Troyte, John Edward, Through The Ranks to a Commission, 1881, MacMillan and Co., London.

BBC, http://www.bbc.co.uk/ww2peopleswar/stories/33/a1166933.shtml BBC World War 2, A People's War [Accessed June 2010]

Baker, 1978, The Rise of the Victorian Actor, Rowman & Littlefield

Bennett, F. West Bromwich Theatre Royal, Bennett, Burton-on-Trent

British Listed Buildings, http://www.britishlistedbuildings.co.uk/en-392565-united-reform-church-lutterworth [accessed 25th November 2010]

Browning, C.A., 1847. The convict ship and England's exiles: in two parts, Hamilton, Adams.

Chancellor, V.E., Master and Artisan in Victorian England, Joseph Gutteridge 1816-1899 and William Andrews 1835-1914.

City of Coventry, The - Crafts and industries: Modern industry and trade | British History Online. Available at: http://www.british-history.ac.uk/report.aspx?compid=16026&strquery=ribbons [Accessed June 3, 2010].

City of Coventry, The - Local government and public services: Public services | British History Online. Available at: http://www.british-history.ac.uk/report.aspx?compid=16035 [Accessed June 4, 2010].

Coventry Evening Telegraph, June 15th 2002, David McGrory.

Daily Life in Victorian England Daily Life Through History: Amazon.co.uk: Sally Mitchell [Accessed June 8, 2010].

Duffin, J., 1996. Soldiers' Work; Soldiers' Health: Morbidity, Mortality, and Their Causes in an 1840s British Garrison in Canada. Labour /Le Travail, 37, 37-80.

Era, The, March 1842. Available at: http://find.galegroup.com.libezproxy.open.ac.uk [Accessed July 2010]

Gateway Prison, St Albans - Retired Prisons on Waymarking.com. Available at: http://www.waymarking.com/waymarks/WM7GP9_Gateway_Prison_St_Albans [Accessed May 31, 2010].

Gentleman's Magazine, The, April 1860, p. 408

Hulk Prisoner. Available at: http://www.kenscott.com/prisons/prisonerexp.htm [Accessed June 22, 2010].

Intolerable Hulks. Available at: http://intolerablehulks.com/intro.html [Accessed June 22, 2010].

Joseph Marie Jacquard: Biography of Joseph Marie Jacquard. Available at: http://www.sacklunch.net/biography/J/JosephMarieJacquard_1.html [Accessed June 4, 2010].

John Bull (London, England), Monday, October 22, 1832; pg. 339; Issue 619. New Readerships.

Kuper, Adam, Kissing Cousins, Newhumanist.org.uk Volume 12 Issue 5 September/October 2009, [accessed 20/11/2010].

Matthew, H.C.G. & Harrison, B. eds., 2004. The Oxford Dictionary of National Biography, Oxford: Oxford University Press. Available at: http://oxforddnb.com/articles/11/11767-article.html?back=#cosubject_11767 [Accessed June 16, 2010].

Neill, S., 2006, Ribbon weaving. Available at: http://www2.warwick.ac.uk/fac/soc/wie/neothemi/pavilionlinks/sent/ [Accessed June 3, 2010].

Radcliffe, J.N., "On the Prevalence of Suicide in England" Transactions of the National Association for the Promotion of Social Science (London, 1862), 465.

Reports of Artisans selected by a committee appointed by the council of the Society of Arts to visit the Paris Universal Exhibition, 1867. Printed by W. Trounce, London.

Sadlers Wells Theatre history, http://www.sadlerswells.com/ [accessed August 2010]

Scoop Database of Journalists, http://www.scoop-database.com/bio/rainbow_edwin [Accessed June 2010]

Strachan, H., 1984. Wellington's legacy: the reform of the British Army, 1830-54, Manchester University Press ND.

Theatreland, London Metropolitan Archives, http://www.cityoflondon.gov.uk/corporation/lma_learning/theatrelands/images.asp [accessed June 2010]

Trevelyan, C.E., 1867. The purchase system in the British army. Available at: http://www.jstor.org.libezproxy.open.ac.uk/stable/60243400 [Accessed June 8, 2010].

Workers and Thinkers, 1896, The American Journal of Sociology, 1(5), 643-652.

Woven Threads Project Research. Available at: http://www.woventhreadsproject.co.uk/research [Accessed June 3, 2010].

Index

6th Battalion of King's Royal Rifles Corp	130
7th Hussars	37
14th Light Dragoons	37
34th Regiment of the Foot	49, 53

A

Acland-Troyte	54
John Edward	50
Act of Uniformity	26
Actor's Association	130
Alcott	
Thomas, Alderman	95
Amner	
John	24
Amott	
Annie	101
Arcenciel	10
Armson	
William	24
Australia	79
Aynsleigh	
Harry	131

B

Bablake	135
Bablake Hospital	135
Ballard	
Emma	149
Barr	
Elizabeth	149
barrack room	50
Basle	42
Bass Strait	79
Bateman	
Kate	112
Battle of Culloden	16
Baxter	
Jas.	89
Beck	
Josiah	36, 37
Bedfordshire	16
Bennett	
Elizabeth	91
Fred	111
Beresford	

Frank	128
Berwick	
Priscilla. *See* Lane: Priscilla	
Birmingham	
Essex Street	105
Mr Blagg	64
Blakesley	
Robert	69
Bohemia	137
Book of Common Prayer	26
Booth	
Mary Ann. *See* Matthews: Mary Ann	
Boyce	
James	79
Bradford	
Elizabeth	29
Elizabeth Bradford (nee Rainbow). *See* Rainbow	
Sarah	29
Thomas	29
Braunstone, Daventry	18
Bray	
Charles	139
Bridgfoot	
Henry	85
British Government	81
British Institute of Journalists	137
Brixham	169
Brown	
Ann	97
Joseph	87
Browne	
Horace	90
Browning	
Colin A.	74
Brundle	
Charles Henry	100
Eliza Ann	94
Elizabeth. *See* Rainbow: Elizabeth	
Louisa	91, 92, 95, 100
William	93, 94
Burberry	
Thomas	37
Bury	123
Star Theatre	109
Busby	
Sabrina	105
Button	
Henry	101

C

Callaghan	
Owen	89
Calvert	
Mary. *See* Tickner: Mary	
Cambridgeshire	
Ramsey	85
Canada	
Quebec	53
Cannon	
Joseph	158
Carlyle	
Vincent W.	130
The Cascades	86
Cash brothers	38
Catholics	39
cat o'nine tails	78
chandler	29
Bonnie Prince Charlie	16
chemist	149
cholera	40
Church of Christ	
Lutterworth	26
Church Wardens	20, 21
Clements	
Ada. *See* Rainbow: Ada	
Cobden Treaty	41
coffee house keeper	40
Coles	
J.	58
Colorado	
Denver	
The Windsor Hotel,	127
Combe	
Charles	128
Comer	
George	110
Conditional Pardon	86
Constable	19, 21
convict record	71, 81
Conway	
F.B.	127
Cotesbach	16, 17, 18, 21, 24, 25, 29
Cotesbach Educational Trust	17, 19
Cotesbach Estate	18
Coulson	
Elizabeth	143

Coventry	10, 33, 36
Barker Butts Secondary School	173
Blitz	167
Bond Hospital	37
Buckingham Rise, Allesley Park,	169
Cash's Lane,	149
Castle Street,	158
Cheveral Avenue, Radford	170
Cow Lane	48
East Street	43
Gosford Street	38
Grangemouth Drive	174
Herbert Art Gallery and Museum	137
High Street	38, 133
Hillfields	39
Lincoln Street	144
Little Park Street	37
London Road Allotments Limited	154
Market Street,	143
New Buildings	37
Queen's Road	140
Queen's Road Baptist church	161
Queen Street	40
Queen Victoria Road	165
Sandy Lane,	172
Silver Street	48
St. John's Church	135
Victoria Street	151
Waverley Road	161
Weston Street	43
Wheatley Street,	170
Coventry Allotment Society	149
Coventry Boy's Brigade	161
Coventry City councillor	149
Coventry Evening Telegraph	138
Coventry Herald	139
Coventry School of Arts	136
Coventry Technical College	136
Department of Science and Art	137
Cox	
Sophia	29
Crewe	
Lyceum Theatre	110
Crick	24
Crofts	
Mary	38
Curzons	
Henry Louis	153

Kitty 48, 153, 177

D

Darlington 112
Darwin
 Charles 30
 George 30
De Burgh
 Marie 128
Deptford 73
Devon 9, 10
Dey
 Barbara 138
Dickens
 Charles 33
Digby
 Maude 128
Douglas
 Mr 64
Dover 49, 53
D'Oyly Carte 117
Dublin
 Fontenoy Street, 157
 Philsborough Baptist Church 157

E

Earl Grey 75
The Earl Grey 74. *See also* prison ship
Eastcheap murder 69
East London Theatre 108
East Lynne 108
Education Act 150
Edward II 135
Enclosure Riots 17
Era
 The 61
The Era 106
Essex Standard 85
Examiner, The, London 59

F

farmer 43
Farmer
 Thomas 25
first cousin marriage 29
flogging 49

Forde
  Fenton   128
Foxall
  Richard   58, 60
Foxhall
  Richard   59
France   39
Franklin
  John, Sir   77, 81
Freedom of the City of Prague   139
Frohman
  Charles   125

G

George Town   86
ginger beer   65
The Girl Who Wouldn't Marry   131
Gladstone
  William   43
Grace
  Amy   128
grazier   26
grazing rights   20
Green
  Sarah   40
The Guardian   137
Gunton
  James   92
Gurney
  Baron   58
  Baron Gurney   68
Gutteridge
  Joseph   41, 42

H

Hamlet   128
Hampshire
  Dover   55
  Gosport   53
  Portsmouth   53
The Hampshire Advertiser   69
Dr Hardy   95
Hayton
  Howard   94
Headquarter Recruit   55
Henry VIII   20, 29
Hertford Assizes   66

Highways Act	23
Hill	
John	24
Hinton	
Ann	40
Sarah	36, 44
His Child Wife	131
Hobart	73
Adelaide Street	88
Bell Street, New Town	99
Cornelian Bay Cemetary	97
Cornelian Bay Railway	95
Davey Street	88
Domain	95
Elizabeth Street	95
Post Office	87
Risdon Road	97
The Hobart Town Daily Mercury	89
Hobart Mercury	87
Hobart Town Advertiser	88
Hodgson	
Hulo	128
Home Guard	165
homosexuality	82
Huguenots	10, 39, 138
hulk	73
Hurst	
Ruth	16, 33

I

IGI	58
Impression Bay	80, 81
In The Dead of Night	113
Iraq	
RAF Habbaniya	167
Irving	
Henry, Sir	130
Isle of Skye	16

J

Jackson	
William Berwick	158
Jacobite Rising	16
Jacquard	
Joseph-Marie	39
Jacquard looms	39
King James I	17

Jeffery	
Graham	48
Jeffs	
Linda	134
Jones	
C.	58
Huw	137
Journalism	56
Joyce	
Percy	175
Justices of the Peace	20
Justitia	73

K

Kinder	
J.	58
Kirk	
Esther	33, 44
Jabez. *See also* Jabez Rainbow	
Kuper	
Adam	30

L

Lacy	
John, PC	60
Ladywood	
Birmingham	158
Lane	
Amy Elizabeth	157
Christina	159
Fred	128
Henry	158
Hubert F.	159
Jabez	158
Margaret	159
Mathew Henry	157
Priscilla	158
Thomas	159
Thomas (Tommy)	158
Launceston	86
Launceston Examiner	101
lawyer's clerk	33
Leamington Spa	171
Cadena Cafe	171
Leeds	
Grafton Street	105
Leicester	21

Southampton Street   106
Leicester Record Office, Wigston   16
Leicestershire   16
The Leonard Rayne and Alfred Paumier company   128
Leonard Rainbow   165–168
Levy
  Jules   127
  Marianne (Minnie)   127
Liberal   42
Light and Shadows in the life of an Artisan, Gutteridge   42
Lillian
  Carlyle. *See* Rainbow: Lillie Blanche
  Herries. *See* Rainbow: Lillie Blanche
Lillingtstone
  Daniel   87
Lipscombe
  J. T.   58
London
  Fawcett Street, Redcliffe Gardens,   119
  Holborn
    National Hospital, Queen Square   131
  Kenton Road, Bloomsbury   176
  St. Augustine's Road, St. Pancras   176
  St. Martin's Lane   40
  Tottenham Court Road   176
Lucan
  Cooldrinagh,   159
Lucky Star   110
Lutterworth   16, 25, 30
Lutterworth Independent Church.   16
Lydekker
  Mr   58

M

Madeira   77
magpie uniform   74
The Main Hope   110
Marriott
  Revd. Robert   18
  Rev. Robert   17
  Robert   18
Marylebone Theatre   108
Matthews
  Edward C.   113
  John   136
  Mary Ann   136
Maycock

Eliza	85
McGregor	
Allan	89
Middlesbrough	122
Midget Minstrels	114
Militia	21
Molesworth	
Isaac	48
Montague	
Herbert J.	129
The Morning Chronicle	71
Motor Neurone Disease	131
Mr Musek	138
Musek	
Pan Karel	138

N

Napoleon III	42
Nelson	
Lord	63
Newcastle on Tyne	129
Newcastle under Lyme	
Albert Street,	131
Newmarket	
Clifton House,	158
Newspaper Press Fund	137
Newton	
Sophy	177
Newton, Northamptonshire	17
New Zealand	94
Northampton	16

O

Open University	47
Ordnance department	50
Ormsby	
Mabel	128
Osbaldiston	
F. J.	58
Othello	128
The Outcasts	108
Overseer of the Highways	24
Overseer of the Poor	19, 20, 21
Oxford	50
Adderbury	91

P

Paignton	169
pantomimes	109
Paris World Exposition	42
Passive Resistance movement	150
Paumier	
Alfred	128
pay for a soldier	53
Dr Payne	96
Pearce	
James	67
Jane	58. See also Pearse
John	67
Joseph	58
Sarah	58
Pearse	
Jane	56, 57, 58–69
penny-a-liners	56
Plummer	
John	88
Poor Relief	21
Port Arthur	80
Portsmouth	73
Post Office	88
Prague	139
Royal Bohemian National Theatre	138
Preyimbula	80
prison ship	74
prostitute	59
Protestant	39
Proved True	110
Prudential Assurance Company	168

Q

Queen Isabella	135
Queen's shilling	54
Queen Victoria's Jubilee celebrations	139

R

Rainbow	
Ada	138
Amy Alice Watts	72, 143, 145–146
Amy Elizabeth. See Lane: Amy Elizabeth	
Charles Edwin	136
Dorothy	149
Edward, Bishop of Carlisle	145
Edwin	10, 38, 40, 133–140
Elizabeth	29, 91, 92, 94. See also Coulson: Elizabeth; See also Barr: Elizabeth

Emma	107–124. *See also* Ballard: Emma
Emma Sarah. *See* Watts: Emma Sarah	
Frank	165
Frank Watts	143
Frederick	29
Hannah	34, 48
Harriet	38, 40
Harry	136, 138
Harry Watts	143
Henry	38, 143–144, 149
Herbert	134
Hilda	165
Jabez	11, 34, 47–90, 102
Jacob	34
James	34, 36, 37, 40, 42
J.G. (Joseph George)	105–123
Job	34, 40
John	16, 24, 26, 34
Joseph	33, 34, 38, 40, 71
not related	91
Joshua	34
Josiah	40
Leonard and Hilda	9
Lillian. *See* Rainbow: Lillie Blanche	
Lillie Blanche	109–131
Mary	16, 25
Olive Edith	149
Patricia	170–174
Percy Leonard	136, 157–162
Sarah	16, 25, 42, 175
Sarah Elizabeth	40
Susan S. Watts	143
William	15, 16, 19, 25, 38, 149
William Ballard	149–153
rations	53
Raven	
Joseph	153
Raynbow	
William. *See* Rainbow, William	
Rayne	
Leonard	128
razor	65
Registrar of Births & Deaths	136
Regulations for Penal Settlements	80
Rex v the inhabitants of Cotesbach	24
ribbon weaving	38
Richardson	
Matthew	58

Mr Riddoch	97
Riot Act	37
Robespierre	130
Robinson	
Robert	64
Romford	119
Ross	86
Rowe	
Mary Alice	125
Royal Theatre, Bristol,	131
Rumball	
J. H.	58

S

Sadler's Wells theatre	107
Mark Sanders	9
Saunders	
Alexander	97
The Savoy	117
Dr Scott	96
Scott	
Mr	58
Sea Queen. *See* prison ship	
Settlement Act of 1662	21
Seven Corporal Works of Mercy	19
Sharman	
Emma Jane. *See* Rainbow: Emma	
Shawell	16, 25, 178
She Stoops To Conquer	113
Shoreditch	36, 44
silk weaver	49
silk weaving	36
silk weaving industry in Coventry	39
Silver War Badge	130
Skinner	
Robert	67
smart money	54
Smith	
J.	58
Society of Arts	42
South Africa	
Cape Town	127
Johannesburg	127
Johannesburg Sportman and Dramatic News	128
Sparkes	
Benjamin	37
Special Sessions	23

Spitalfields	44
Spittalfields	138
SS Moor	128
St. Albans	47, 53, 56
Christopher Yard	64
High Street	64
The Boot	62
The Boot public house	59
Town Hall	62
White Lion	59
The Star, Wolverhampton	115
St. Catherine's Church, Coventry	36
St. Etienne	42
Sudden Arrhythmic Death Syndrome	100
Surveyor of the Highways	23
The Susan	74, 76. *See also* prison ship
Swaysland	
Stephen	87

T

Tasman	
Abel	79
Tasmania	72, 79, 91
Taylor	
Jane	85
Phoebe	16
Tearle	
Beatrice	125
Conway	130
George Osmond	125
Mary. *See* Rowe: Mary Alice	
Osmond	125–129
Temperance Society	77
Thames	73
Theatre Royal Birmingham	108
Theatre Royal Grimsby	108
Theatre Royal, West Bromwich	111
Theresa	75. *See also* prison ship
The Shadows on the Blind	113
Thorpe	
Robert	58
'Through The Ranks to a Commission', Ackland-Troyte	50
Ticket of Leave	81, 86
Tickner	
George	88
Mary	88
The Times	57, 64, 67

Chasing Rainbows

Times Digital Archives	11
Toogood	
Alfred	37
top shop	39
transported	68
Trevelyan	
Charles, Sir	55
triangle	78
Trindle	
John	153

U

undertaker	39
United Reform Church	
Lutterworth	26
USA	
New York	145

V

Van Diemen's Land	37, 57, 71, 73, 79
Vereker	
Sydney	128
Detective Vickers	90

W

Walker	
James	87
Walks Thru' Coventry	139
Walley	
John	87
Wallick	
Lester	125
Warwick	
All Saint's Church, Emscote,	165
Emscote Road	161
Humphriss Street,	170
Old Square,	161
Smith Street	161
Warwickshire	
Lighthorne,	172
Watts	
Emma Sarah	143
Webster	
Richard	58, 62–68
Weldon	
Christy	159
West	

John	79
West Bromwich Albion	114
Wheatley	
Thomas	135
Whitbread	
William	90
White	
Joseph	67
Whitley Bay	129
Who Do You Think You Are	15
Wilkins	
Hilda. *See* Rainbow: Hilda	
Williams	
Charles	89
Wolverhampton	
Cleveland Street	110
Wood's Tasmanian Almanack	87
Woolwich	74
Royal Arsenal docks	73
workhouse	67
World War I	130

Chasing Rainbows

Made in the USA
Charleston, SC
02 June 2011